EVERY LEADER'S EVEREST

EVERY LEADER'S EVEREST

Ascending From
Insecurity to Identity

JIM C. MOLLOY

Contact Jim:
www.LeaderScripts.com

Yet if you devote your heart to him
and stretch out your hands to him,
if you put away the sin that is in your hand
and allow no evil to dwell in your tent,
then you will lift up your face without shame;
you will stand firm and without fear.
You will surely forget your trouble,
recalling it only as waters gone by.
Life will be brighter than noonday,
and darkness will become like morning.
***You will be secure**, because there is hope;*
you will look about you and take your rest in safety.
You will lie down, with no one to make you afraid,
and many will court your favor.

(Job 11:13–19)

CONTENTS

DEDICATION

For Sandy,

Many waters cannot quench love;
rivers cannot wash it away.
(Song of Solomon 8:7)

Refreshing streams, angry rivers;
Familiar tides, anxious currents;
Peaceful ebbs, fierce flows;
Gentle pools, tiring rapids.
Charts in error, Lying stars misguide,
Lost, hands held together;
Tossed often, still tethered fast;
Ceaseless grasp,
Endless love.

THANKS

Thank you Rebecca, my former assistant, for your work on the original manuscript. I forgive you for leaving me to be closer to your family. I forgive you, but I'm not over it.

Thank you Linette, for tirelessly reading and rereading this over and over without complaining. Their is no proofreder like your.

Thank you Sandy, for all of your patience through all my projects and whims. As H.G. Wells said, "She stuck to me so sturdily that in the end I stuck to myself."

Thank you Mom, Dad, Pam, Lyle, Goward, Clara, Mikayla, and Noah. I know family doesn't really have a choice, but thanks for your love anyway.

Thank you Jake, Ethan, and Brody for being boys that a dad couldn't be more proud of. (Except when you mark on newly painted walls, miss the toilet, or sprain your ankle on a dirt bike. But even then, I love you guys.)

Thank you Pastor Doug, for being a great friend, mentor and a model of secure leadership.

Thank you colleagues and coworkers, for adding spice and fun to life. It is an honour to serve our district and country with you.

Thank you to those who said, "You can do it." When you said "Your book will be awesome," I knew you were lying, but it still felt good.

Thank you Jesus, for the blessings listed above.

PREFACE

S cattered on the slopes of the highest mountain on planet earth there are dead bodies. They serve as a gruesome reminder of the hazards of climbing Mount Everest. Of the 189 people who have died, 120 of them still lie there. It is too risky to bring their bodies back down. The natural peril of the "death zone" (the area between the last base camp at 26,000 feet and the peak) is too much to overcome.

Not every leader makes it to the top. But I'm praying that as you read these pages you will feel the Holy Spirit's push upward, onward, and forward. May He be the oxygen in your climbing tank and His presence, power, and purposes be sufficient to assist you on your climb to security and identity.

For leaders, achievement is both a blessing and a curse. It is first a blessing because we have been mandated to bear fruit and to be effective. Secondly, it can be a curse. When we are insecure our victories, even the shallowest ones, feel substantial because of our unhealthy drive to achieve. Today, we are applauded for what we do, not what we are becoming. So we seek the next big gig and the next dramatic moment. Cursed to swing to the next vine of achievement, we make our way through the jungle, forgetting who we are and becoming unable to rest.

All leaders, especially successful ones, are tempted to assume that they are the sum of what they can produce. In the end, insecurity always lowers our expectations and changes our estimation of what we really consider as success. We begin to count numbers, trophies, and performances, at the expense of transformed people. People become tools to our success but they are supposed to be the targets of our investment. We begin to celebrate the wrong things. We settle for flash without substance.

The most difficult journeys in leadership often require us to peer deep inside of ourselves, to make adjustments, and face those inner realities that influence the way we lead. This book invites you on such a voyage. *Every Leader's Everest* will give you the keys to address your own insecurity, and it will prepare you to help those you lead to overcome their insecurity as well. Soul renovation only happens by hard conversations, attention to the inner parts of self, and Holy Spirit conviction.

Thank you, reader, for spending some of your valuable hours with me. There are many other books out there and you chose this one. I pray that I do you no dissatisfaction with these pages. Please engage in an e-conversation with me by visiting my website.

Blessings upon you as you read and climb!

Jim Molloy

FOREWORD

Through this timely book, Jim presents a relevant, practical, and scripturally grounded approach to the haunting issue of insecurity. Many of us have felt or know someone who has faced the inner churning of insecurity, particularly when having met a new challenge or a path not yet walked.

Dr. Norman Vincent Peale wrote an article almost thirty years ago titled "Imagine Your Way to Confidence." He wrote, "Imagine yourself succeeding in the area where you wish most completely for success." Often the area in which we wish to succeed greatest relates to general acceptance. Jim, with a twist of viewpoint, lays out for us a solid biblical path to security in this area: Living from or out of acceptance rather than for acceptance. The foundational truth is that we are accepted first by and through Christ's sacrifice for all mankind, and then we can live from his acceptance rather than for acceptance.

Jim cannot be defined as just a theorist. As an early mentor, friend, and colleague of Jim's for almost twenty years, I am very comfortable stating that he discovered and lived out the wisdom he shares with us in this book. The young people he served in the early to mid-nineties are now well into adulthood, yet whenever their paths cross with Jim they always address him as "Pastor Jim." This warm greeting stems from their incredible respect and honour for their former leader and mentor who, among other things, encouraged them to be secure in Christ and accept, with confidence, the challenge that each tomorrow brings. Like Moses, these young people would balk, but with Jim's assuring nudge they ventured with confidence into uncharted waters and foreign challenges. Eventually Jim's words; —"I need your help, you can do it"—became marching orders for these young future leaders.

Jim believes people are formed in Christ's image and, when encouraged to trust in Him, will enjoy a fulfilling life of security and success.

Insecurity doesn't stay stagnant but, if not addressed, can grow like entangling weeds, eventually blinding vision, darkening life, and choking energy and spirit. There is a path out of insecurity's grip, which leads us to an inner posture of security. I believe this book presents sound, tried, and attainable ways of taking the "in" out of insecurity and allowing "security" to define every person who will choose to "live *out* of security rather than *for* security."

I highly recommend this book to you and trust you feel confident in my endorsement. Enjoy the ride as you take the "in" out of *insecurity*.

Rev. R. Douglas Moore
Superintendent, Maritime District
Pentecostal Assemblies of Canada

1

INSECURITY

W e didn't know our son was significantly deaf until he was about three years old. Unknown to us at the time, Jake had Enlarged Vestibular Aqueduct Syndrome. EVAS is a form of hearing loss caused by the enlargement of the vestibular aqueduct in the inner ear. It is one of the most common inner ear deformities resulting in hearing loss.

As a toddler, Jake learned to follow instructions by catching various cues, like hearing the word "teeth" and understanding that it was time to brush his teeth. He even developed the ability to lip-read at a basic level—a skill that he used as a child and still uses as a teen whenever eavesdropping is required.

I remember taking our little preschooler to get his hearing tested. Despite his vehement denial of any hearing loss, the test confirmed that he had a binaural deficiency. Moulds were taken of his ear canals and hearing aids were ordered.

A few weeks later, we returned to the audiologist to try them. It was a sunny Wednesday morning in downtown Halifax. The streets were congested and the air held the dull roar of rush hour. I parked the car and headed across the street into the clinic, little boy in tow. Up the elevator. Through the corridors. Past the fish tank. Across the playroom. Into the audiologist's office.

She fitted the devices into his ears and asked me to go down the corridor and around the corner. From that distance I spoke, "Jake, can you hear me?"

Jake responded with excitement, "Dad! These walkie-talkies are great!" He was still convinced his hearing was fine, believing that the devices were only providing transmission, not amplification.

Leaving the office, we crossed the street towards our car. Jake suddenly jolted and grabbed my leg! A large truck was downshifting further up the street, but his new hearing aids made him think that the truck was upon him.

Parked further ahead was a shiny black Mustang convertible. Jake's dream car.

"Look, Jake! A black convertible!"

Jake burst into silly laughter. "Ha! You're funny, Daddy!"

It is common for my children to laugh at me, but I was still confused. "Why are you laughing at me? Why is Daddy funny?"

He giggled. "Daddy, it's not a 'convertible.' It's a 'vertible'!" And as we debated the car type on the sidewalk of a busy street, I realized that he had never heard the "con" part of "convertible" before, and had never known it was missing.

Every leader is tempted at some point to switch into autopilot and stop engaging in new tasks or trying new things. The "con" has been absent so long that they doubt there actually is anything else. I have also met leaders who are convinced the situations and challenges they face have little to do with them. They are deaf to their own issues and insecurity (or at least they pretend to be). As a leader I have discovered that sometimes the problem has been *me*. Looking deeper, I have found that unheard (or unacknowledged) sounds in my life have more impact than I would like to admit.

Do you have that nagging sensation that something is not quite right or an awareness that something is a little off? There couldn't possibly be something else, could there? I'm guessing that God has something more for you, your life, and your leadership. What role is insecurity playing in your life and leadership? What sound frequency must you tune into to hear the impact insecurity is having on you? For some, it has always been '"vertible.' Perhaps there are some tones of your understanding that remain unheard too?

We do not appreciate how damaging the absence of these frequencies are until the other clatter gets too loud to ignore. Most of us are unaware of the extent of all of this because we lack objectivity. Robert McGee writes:

> Human beings develop elaborate defense mechanisms to block pain and gain significance. We suppress emotions; we are compulsive protectionists; we drive ourselves to succeed, or we withdraw and become passive; we attack people who hurt us; we punish ourselves when we fail; we try to say clever things to be accepted; we help people so that we will be appreciated; and we say and do countless other things.[1]

Consequently, as we sometimes do with a beeping smoke detector, we pull out the battery and spend our next days in danger.

We all wear camouflage, thinking, "If people don't see the real me, they can't hurt the real me." Assessing this insecurity leads us down a long and difficult process—one that might require uncomfortable and difficult transformation. Let's walk through these next chapters together with an eye to the role insecurity might be playing in our ability to be effective leaders and develop successful relationships. This might hurt a bit, but the payoff will be worth it.

Though we might not recognize its influence, insecurity threatens our most primal needs, including our need to be valued. Lawrence Crabb wrote, "The basic personal need of each person is to regard himself as a worthwhile human being."[2]

Everyone has insecurity, but no one is born insecure. It is a learned trait. One may be born soft-hearted or sensitive, but insecurity is developed as a person grows, emerging and evolving in different ways throughout the various stages of life. We must determine how significantly insecurity affects us and whether or not it is becoming dysfunctional or debilitating in its intensity.

The term "insecurity" is bigger than implying that someone lacks confidence or self-assurance. It steps beyond uncertainty and anxiety. Originating in the seventeenth century, the word insecurity comes from Medieval Latin, from "in" (meaning "not") plus "securus" (meaning "free from care"). Therefore the word is best interpreted as "not free from care" or, as some suggest "unsafe." Insecure people can be dangerous leaders to follow.

In *The Tender Heart*, Dr. Joseph Nowinski writes:

> The word insecurity has a particular meaning, and a particular cause. Insecurity refers to a profound sense of self-doubt—a deep feeling of uncertainty about our basic worth and our place in the world. Insecurity is associated with chronic self-consciousness, along with a chronic lack of confidence in ourselves and anxiety about our relationships. The insecure man or woman lives in constant fear of rejection and a deep uncertainty about whether his or her own feelings and desires are legitimate.[3]

The intensity of our insecurity directly affects how we view the world and how we respond to life's blessings and problems. It influences our reaction to conflict, criticism, and loss. It even shapes our interpretation of praise and admiration when we are affirmed. If we get too excited by praise, we become devastated by criticism. Nowinski further suggests:

> The insecure person also harbors unrealistic expectations about love and relationships. These expectations, for themselves and for others, are often unconscious. The insecure person creates a situation in which being disappointed and hurt in relationships is almost inevitable. Ironically, although insecure people are easily and frequently hurt, they are usually unaware of how they are unwitting accomplices in creating their own misery.[4]

We will explore all of this in more detail in later chapters, but a simple metaphor might help. Think of insecurity as an automobile. The fuel that powers it is *unrealistic expectation*. Unrealistic expectation is the catalyst for all insecurity because the more you try to become what you think you ought to be, the further you get from being who you are meant to be.

The ignition is *past experiences*. Life's successes and failures, one's background or upbringing, are what start the insecurity process or contribute to how insecurity will be manifested.

The accelerator pedal, then, is *disposition*. The natural personality and demeanour of a person mixes with their experiences and their current state to accelerate uncertainty. Different dispositions and personalities cause the variance in the display of insecurity.

Sitting in the passenger seat is *jealousy*, an evil co-pilot, ready to navigate insecurity to dangerous places. The back seat passengers are *rejection and loss*. These guys are along to assist in spurring insecurity and making sure that even an outgoing or seemingly confident person remains insecure.

Pop the hood and you'll see *lack of belief in one's acceptance* by the Creator. As Lloyd Ogilvie suggests, "All insecurity is rooted in an inadequate sense of belonging to God."[5] Our problem is not a low view of ourselves, it's that we have too low a view of God.

Good looks, wealth, prestige, or power cannot bring the refuge we seek. At the end of all our journeying, we have only to discover that *the Lord is our security*. When we feel **insecure**, what we are really feeling is **fear**. Insecurity *is* fear. Unhealthy fear is always the result of a lie. Dr. Chris Thurman writes,

> Every lie that goes through your mind is slow, self-inflicted psycho-logical and spiritual death. Every lie you think costs you your life. The lies we believe are the mental bullets that kill our souls, and they inflict significant damage often without our even realizing it until it is too late.[6]

Like you, I have been afraid too. In many ways, I still am. I am writing this book not only because I have studied the psychology of insecurity, but because I have lived in its grip.

• • •

The whole world suffers the loss of artists' contributions when insecurity wins. Humankind never sees their masterpieces. Ears never hear their unwritten symphonies. Insecurity is the reason there are singers who do not sing and writers who do not write.

Insecurity visits everyone. I fight it every day. So do you.

Insecurity lies. It always lies. It only lies.

Insecurity makes us into fools.

Insecurity is a bully.

Insecurity is powerless. It needs the fuel we feed it.

Insecurity doesn't care or empathize.

Insecurity seeks not to injure but to annihilate.

Insecurity tells us to "sit down, shut up, and do nothing."

Insecurity runs scared when we threaten to become the people we are meant to be and we do that for which we are called.

Insecurity is scared to be alone.

Insecurity cannot be touched, smelled, or held. It can only be felt. It is always damaging, depressing, and disapproving. It is evil.

Insecurity lives on the inside. It cannot be banished by medication. It is the foe within. Only Jesus can drive it out.

Insecurity seeks to drop us down a level, never to lift us to a higher rung. It always leads to regression, never progress. It always weakens and never empowers.

Insecurity is a bad habit.

Insecurity teaches us to put off, postpone, and procrastinate.

Insecurity's best friend is Criticism. Its lover is Judgmentalism.

Insecurity likes drama. It is the father of trouble and the mother of distraction. It tempts and teaches us to be victims. (After all, who can expect much from us if we are miserable? Misfortune is such a wonderful excuse.)

Insecurity tells us that we must be free of fear in order to achieve anything. Security knows that being "free of fear" is an illusion. There is no such thing as a "fearless leader" and the ones who try to appear fearless are idiots.

Insecurity is not defeated by a great relationship, financial success, popularity, recaptured youth, beauty, power, or prestige.

Insecurity cannot be destroyed, but it can surely be dominated.

Imagine what would happen if insecurity fled. Alcohol companies would dry up. Drug trafficking would halt. Self-help books would become history, as would plastic surgery, Botox, and marijuana. Imagine what wonderful productions would walk across life's stage! What great risks would be taken! What fantastic strides forward!

2

RELIANCE

"Some trust in chariots, and some in horses; but we will make mention of the name of Jehovah our God."

(Psalm 20:7, ASV)

Following a drastic turn and sharp descent, the pilot announced that an emergency landing was necessary. The slight quiver in his voice betrayed his attempt at nonchalance. Just a few minutes earlier, the co-pilot had awkwardly informed us that the right engine was on fire. They shut down the faulty one. He assured the cabin that they were trained and able to fly an aircraft with a single engine.

I had chosen this airline to save a few dollars. It was a new airline with young pilots and an even younger crew. I was seated in seat 1c on a short night-time flight from Toronto to Ottawa before connecting to another flight that would take me home to my pretty wife and fun-loving kids. Having the closest seat to the cockpit gave me a front-row view of the commotion.

Flight attendants scurried to satisfy all their rehearsed protocols and procedures while trying to reassure a few hundred anxious travelers. Their attempts to soothe passengers failed when another turn, to align the aircraft to the runway, revealed a strip of asphalt flanked on either side by emergency vehicles illuminating the night. Their flashing lights told us, "We fully expect you to crash."

The pilot instructed the crew to take their seats in preparation for "landing." A young attendant took her spot in the jump-seat facing me. Our knees were about four feet apart, leaving little choice but for us to engage in an uncomfortable chitchat. At my best, I'm silly and sarcastic. At my worst, well, I'm just plain awkward.

"Are you okay, sir?" she dutifully asked. She added a nervous smirk.

"Yes, I'm fine. How 'bout you? Are you doing okay?"

"Oh, yes. We are trained to handle this. We learned about this in school."

Trying to be funny, I asked, "So they taught you how to conquer gravity?"

She didn't laugh. I fumbled with a magazine. My seatmate started crying.

In case you are wondering, we did not crash and I did not die. We landed with a vicious thud and an abrupt stop. Emergency vehicles rushed to the aircraft. After a few minutes, we were dispensed like livestock back into the Toronto terminal, and a few hours later I was on another aircraft heading home.

What struck me during this unexpected descent was the constant repetition of the young crew's "education." I suppose that's what we tend to do when we are in a new crisis or have limited experience. We assert our qualifications and credentials. But education can never carry the ball the whole way. It isn't enough. I would rather have heard, "We have been through this a dozen times before. It'll be okay."

I need my surgeon to have diplomas and certificates hung on his office wall, but before he cuts me open I want to know that he has sliced a few dozen people already—and with a high rate of success. I want my chiropractor to have done more than watch a few YouTube training clips. I want those who are responsible for the ones I love to have cultivated some instinct and intuition. They have to bring to the table more than their education.

There is a difference between "education" and "training." In leadership preparation, we may have over-promoted education. Leadership cannot be taught. It is a God-given talent. Skills can be taught, but leadership is not a skill. Nor is it a science. It is an art. It comes from within.

In the ministry context, leadership is empowered by a supernatural force that reaches beyond education. The natural talent of leadership can only be enhanced. Skills and tools can be added. We cannot make leaders, but we can make leaders become better. This is why leadership giftings (and callings) can transcend all personality types, self-esteem, upbringing, and dysfunction. It is also the reason why insecure people can still grow as leaders, regardless of their concept of self. Insecure leaders must learn that when they say it is impossible for them to do what God has asked, it is less a statement about their weakness and more a testimony about their lack of faith in God.

Your path to leadership has made you into the leader you are, and the effects of that journey are often the same things that empower and validate your leadership. Ability is the gift of experience, as is intuition, wisdom, knowledge, and confidence. These, therefore, are like gold and should never be squandered. The blessings you have received are always for you to share with others. Likewise, the curses and crosses you have borne are for you to share as well—in the form of warning signs for others. If one's path into leadership is void of obstacles, chances are that the path didn't lead anywhere significant. Without challenges, the reward of arriving at the destination isn't as sweet.

It is precisely these paths which create meaningful leadership. Indeed, there is a deep modern-day thirst for gripping and innovative leadership. People are pleading for leaders who will inspire them to go places they would never go alone and to attempt things they would normally consider unattainable. They want someone who will give them the opportunity to end up somewhere on purpose.

The problem is that none of us are born with the leadership skills we need to help guide those who follow our lead. Our theological institutions have done well with aligning our theology, but they have failed to enhance us as leaders. We are left with a propensity to replicate the poor leadership habits of others, especially when spiritual models and mentors are not easily found.

The root of this crisis is neither cognitive nor academic. It is not church malfunction. It is not institutional apathy. The problem is spiritual, psychological, and yes, in some part theological. Simply, we are scared. I doubt there has ever been an era when leaders have been more timid about who they are or what they are aiming for. Bill Thrall says, "The dysfunctions of many leaders are rooted in a common reality: Their capacities have been extensively trained while their character has been merely presumed."[7] This assumption cultivates and nourishes insecurity.

These insecurities are most evident in those who are incessant workaholics, or those who have resigned themselves to coast lazily through leadership.

We will deal with these more thoroughly in subsequent chapters, but there are initial clues that often point to such insecure leaders:

1. Their conversations center on themselves.
2. They enjoy telling others of their busyness and obligations.
3. Attendance patterns, finances, and the sum of church programs mean more to these church leaders than transformed lives.
4. They have the need to maintain control and they struggle with permitting others to lead, especially if the others lead well or lead better than they do.
5. They feel threatened, jealous, or angry, and display a need to brag or become sarcastic when in the company of a proficient leader.
6. They feel vulnerable when a subordinate outperforms them.
7. They are reluctant to give credit for victories and struggle to celebrate someone else's achievements.
8. They get annoyed when people do not call them by their title.
9. They default to leading by consensus (what people think) rather than in consultation with God.

These attributes cause us to try to master the "how-to's" rather than the "why." In *The Call*, Os Guinness describes the calling as "the truth that God calls us to himself so decisively that everything we are, everything we do, and everything we have is invested with a special devotion and dynamism lived out as a response to his summons and service."[8] However, we are now reducing ourselves to becoming ministry technicians.

Why Are We Insecure?

There are several interrelated and broad explanations as to why we operate so often in insecurity. **First, our understanding of God's love is deficient**. Our striving to prove ourselves, in order to be validated by those around us, clearly communicates that we really do not believe our own teachings about grace.

Insecurity tells us that you are what you do, and if you do not *do*, then you *are* nothing. Yet in fact you are made worthy not by what you do but by the reality that you are a child of God. Therefore, you must not lead **for** acceptance, but **from** acceptance. James Lawrence expresses this in his fantastic book,

Growing Leaders, and continues by saying, "Unless we know we are chosen, the children of a loving God, we will lead from an insecure place, constantly twisting the privilege of a leadership position to meet our own needs."[9]

The Bible says that you are his workmanship. In other words, you are a masterpiece. On one of those antique evaluation shows, people show up with junk and walk away with valuable treasures after an appraiser reveals its true value. Have you ever seen the painting *Dora Maar au Chat*? I have no real understanding of art, but in my opinion it is a creepy image comparable to some of the projects done by school children. However, *Dora Maar au Chat* is worth at least $102 million! The reason? Pablo Picasso painted it. Because of the artist, it is almost priceless.

You have immense worth because of who painted you. His signature is scribed onto you. You may feel low when you consider intelligence, looks, popularity, or ability—but you are "worth more than gold."

Second, we operate in insecurity because we pursue personal agendas rather than follow Jesus. Without a focus on Jesus, our motives for leadership become skewed by our own needs. Our abilities promote us to places where our character cannot keep us. We become victims of our own giftedness. We have clever strategy sessions to formulate creative vision plans without prayer; yet Jesus said, *"Apart from me, you can do nothing"* (John 15:5). Gerald Harrison contends, "Ministry is what we leave in our tracks as we concentrate on following Jesus."[10] We should fix our eyes on the Father.

Leaders must ask, "What is motivating me to do, or not do, the ministries that I am performing?" The motivation question is the most important self-assessment to consider.

Third, we neglect to cultivate an intimate relationship with God. The quantity of ministry confidence we possess is directly related to the depth of our spiritual walk. It is a "first love" issue. *"I know your deeds, your hard work and your perseverance… yet I hold this against you: You have forsaken your first love"* (Revelation 2:2, 4). We are insecure because we know things are not well in our spiritual lives. Some leaders rarely practice spiritual disciplines. We do not pray as we should. The Scriptures have become "for reference only." Solitude is not practiced. Fasting has become obsolete. Repentance seems passé. We are so busy trying to change others that we forget to continually change ourselves.

In contrast, as George Barna writes in *Revolution*, "Revolutionaries zealously pursue an intimate relationship with God, which Jesus promised we could have through Him. They recognize that there is a huge price to pay in this life-time… but an eternal pay-off as well."[11]

Oswald Chambers adds to this truth when he writes, "Beware of anything that competes with loyalty to Jesus Christ, the greatest competitor of devotion to Jesus is service for him… The one aim of the call of God is the satisfaction of God, not a call to do something for him."[12] Knowing and doing His will depends on the substance of our relationship with Him. If our "first love" is not healthy, then nothing else in our lives will be completely healthy, either.

Next, we lack clear purpose and mission. Mother Teresa for example, had a clear mission. She once said, "I am not [made] for meetings and conventions. Speaking in public and I don't agree."[13] She refused to be distracted by the lure of the crowd. Without a clear purpose in life, we are left to work day by day, giving ourselves over to the tyranny of the urgent rather than the important. We bounce from project to project and never get to do that which we were called to do. We try to lay track in front of a moving train. Consequently, we never determine our particular purpose in the Mission. We never figure out our "wiring," our "sweet spot," or our "niche." We become unsure of what we have been called to achieve. We are pushed to a place of doubt.

Chris Gardner, the man behind the story featured in the film *The Pursuit of Happyness*, understood the importance of realizing purpose. He once said, "Find something you love to do so much, you can't wait for the sun to rise to do it all over again."[14]

Lastly, we do not make an effort to resolve our issues. Skeletons remain in the closet. Bad habits go unchallenged. Temptations and tendencies get ignored. The love of money, lust, or power strangles our potential. It is impossible for those held captive to their issues to feel secure. Every prisoner feels the torment of being under the control of something.

Leadership confidence has little to do with theological prowess, management competencies, personality, or skillset. Instead, such security comes from knowing God's love, having clarity of purpose, resolving our issues, and developing closeness with Christ. In the journey toward inner health, insecurity is not defeated by becoming surer about our leadership but rather by being absolutely sure about God.

3
PAIN

My wife, Sandy, was trying to teach our son, Jake, the importance of grammar. She scribbled this phrase on a scrap of paper: "Woman without her man is nothing." Jake was in silent agreement until his mother added punctuation: "Woman: without her, man is nothing." Jake groaned.

Linette, my assistant, is an outstanding proofreader. She has to constantly add or delete my commas. I, stick them, in weird places, and, omit them, where they are necessary. For example, a few months ago my response to a leader's email inquiry was, "We can do whatever I think!" As you would expect, it came across as condescending and arrogant. However, what I meant to say was, "We can do whatever, I think." The elusive comma! Its addition often reveals a statement's intended purpose. The placement of such a pause gives the sentence its meaning and value.

Unwelcomed commas are often jotted into the sentences of our lives. But don't be too quick to reach for that pink eraser. Leave it alone—just for a little while. The comma might just be God dispensing more meaning and value into your life.

By the way, it might be a good idea to jot a little comma into your life yourself. **God has given you enough time in a day to accomplish what He wants of you that day.** If you are too busy *doing* good, you will find no time to *be* good.

A Comma Is Not a Coma

Pain makes us insecure. It is often not the suffering that really bothers us, though. It's the apparent withdrawal of God from our situation. David felt the same way: *"How long, o Lord? Will you forget me forever? How long will you hide your face from me? How long must I wrestle with my thoughts and every day have sorrow in my heart?"* (Psalm 13:1–2)

To be honest, it seems that the hard times in my life have been paired with the absence of *feeling* His presence. I have no answer, and the "Footprints" poem doesn't bring much relief. But after the pain is over, I can look back and see the attendance of the hand of God.

Most good things take a while to ripen, so be patient and trust Him. Your pain will give way to pleasure in season. The story is not over. There is more to come. God is never late, never too early, and always right on time. Soon He will speak the words, "That's enough." The trial that has seized you is common to many people. God is faithful; He will not let you be taken to a place where you can bear it no longer. But when you are suffering, He will provide a way out—in time. You can stand up under the weight of pain. Scripture reminds us that His favour lasts a lifetime. Weeping may remain for a night, but rejoicing comes in the morning.

On a stormy evening when Jesus came walking on the water toward the disciples, Scripture records that they were afraid because they thought he was a ghost. We tend to label that which we don't understand as evil. Jesus was coming to them in a different way—a way they had not seen before. The truth is, Jesus is often hard to recognize in a storm. It is in the darkest moment that we must strain hardest to see light.

Remember, it is just a pause. It's not an end. Do not confuse the Author's grammar. He has not inserted a period; it is just a comma. It's not a stop sign. It's a yield sign. It is just for now. It's not forever. Don't let trouble cause your faith to become rotted and your insecurity to flourish.

A Comma Gives Meaning

It is what comes after the comma that unveils the complete meaning of the sentence. Only after a painful pause can we understand more of His plan. New meaning and focus is found. Fresh purpose is discovered and we learn something about ourselves that we did not know before. You will learn more in a few days of pain than you will in a few years without it. Anyone who comes to Jesus so that their life will be pain-free has misunderstood their conversion.

Paul wrote epistles while stuck in prison. The Israelites were "paused" at the edge of the Red Sea until the crisis gave way to parting waters. John was in the harsh environment of Patmos and yet was *"in the Spirit."* It was during that pause that John, in Revelation 1, heard God's voice, *"like a trumpet,"* which said: *"Write on a scroll what you see and send it to the churches."* Much revelation comes to us in the form of a comma. If we want a demonstration of God's power, we have to have comma times when we are faced with difficult or impossible situations.

These just might be your sweetest days. It might look like the enemy is winning, but what he intended for evil, God meant for good. When it is done, you will thank Him for the experience. Brokenness always makes a pathway to God and, as Henri Nouwen said, our own wounds make us available as a source of healing.[15] The things we go through will eventually serve to relieve the pain that others are enduring.

For example, Jesus' encounter with a blind man in John 9 caused the disciples to ask Him if the sin of the man or his parents caused the blindness. Jesus was quick to teach them that his blindness wasn't the fault of the man or his parents. Rather, he was blind so that *"the works of God might be manifest in him"* John 9:3.

A Comma Protects

Mornings in the Molloy household are chaotic and hectic. Five of us are off in five different directions heading to five different places. In one of these mornings of madness, Sandy informed me that she recently purchased some sort of "organic" toothpaste. ("Organic" is just a fancy way of saying "yucky" and "more expensive.") She showed it to me, but I have always considered myself to be more of a Colgate man. After a few reminders, I agreed to give it a try. I hated it. It tasted awful and made my teeth feel grimy. A few days later, I slowed down my morning rush enough to read the tube: "Tender Tush." I had been brushing my teeth with medicated buttocks ointment for babies.

A comma might get in the way of your "run-on" lifestyle, but it just might be worth the interruption. God might be putting His comma on your life, but it is for your protection and preservation. It is not there to make you feel unsettled or insecure.

> And the God of all grace, who called you to his eternal glory in Christ, after you have suffered a little while, will himself restore you and make you strong, firm and steadfast. (1 Peter 5:10)

A Comma Disciplines

There is no life that is void of difficulty. D.L. Moody once made a declaration of his commitment of service to the Lord. Within a few days of that declaration, both his church and his house burned down. Thornton Wilder, in his play, *The Angel that Troubled the Waters*, wrote, "In Love's service, only the wounded soldiers can serve."[16]

Growing up in the King James world, it used to be called "chastening." We learned that the Lord "chasteneth" those whom He loves. But every leader has likely thought, in error, "God did this because He is angry with what I did." Chastening isn't God's way of getting even; God got even at the cross. Moreover, one can be chastened even when living right (think Job, think Joseph).

Scripture says that God disciplines us for our good, that we may share in his holiness. R.T. Kendall says, "Our suffering has profound and vast implications for the greater Kingdom of God. There are unseen reasons."[17] Paul wrote, *"Therefore I will boast all the more gladly about my weaknesses, so that Christ's power may rest on me. That is why, for Christ's sake, I delight in weaknesses, in insults, in hardships, in persecutions, in difficulties. For when I am weak, then I am strong."* (2 Corinthians 12:9–10).

If you can't fix it, feature it! The writer of Hebrews, referencing a verse in Proverbs, writes, *"My son, do not make light of the Lord's discipline, and do not lose heart when he rebukes you, because the Lord disciplines those he loves, and he punishes everyone he accepts as a son."* (Hebrews 12:5–6). His grace is sufficient for you. God's power is made perfect in your weakness.

What makes a good leader? There are three practical things: preparation, experience, and pain. A leader who hasn't suffered is not worth following. Hope only grows in the soil of pain, and leadership without hope is weakened because leaders live in the hope that things will change. By example they teach their followers to hope for something that has not yet come to pass. Although suffering may cause one to be uneasy, unsure, and insecure, it plays an important role in leadership. That which is driving a leader to become insecure is often the same thing that propels his or her capability. In other words, the harder the breeze, the stronger the trees.

The story of Joseph helps explain the link between security and suffering (see Genesis 37–50).

Joseph was hated so much by his brothers that he was sold off into slavery. Afterward, he lived with flawless integrity, but his boss, after believing a lie about him, tossed him in jail. If that wasn't bad enough, someone then broke a promise and, as a result, he spent years in captivity. He suffered mentally, relationally, and physically. Yet at the time of his father's death, Joseph revealed his profound understanding of pain:

> His brothers then came and threw themselves down before him. "We are your slaves," they said.
>
> But Joseph said to them, "Don't be afraid. Am I in the place of God? You intended to harm me, but God intended it for good to accomplish what is now being done, the saving of many lives. So then, don't be afraid. I will provide for you and your children."
>
> And he reassured them and spoke kindly to them. (Genesis 50:18–21)

As Joseph responded to suffering with faith, meekness, and humility, God moulded and shaped a leader. Rich lessons, through pain, catapulted Joseph into a high level of leadership competence and emotional security. Remember, the young Joseph dealt with his insecurity by bragging to his brothers and his father about the visions God gave him. Even though Joseph's brothers were undoubtedly wrong in their actions, Joseph himself had much to learn about humility.

In Genesis 39:2–6, we see Joseph learning how to serve and be faithful. Genesis 39:7–20 reveals his standard of moral purity. He learns the lesson of patience in Genesis 40:1–14, 23. Multiple times he is enabled to see God accomplish His purposes and fulfill His promises. In the end, He *saves many lives.* "People often meet their destiny on the road they take to avoid it," says one French proverb. It was A. W. Tozer who said, "Whom God would use greatly, He will hurt deeply."

Charles C. West said, "We turn to God for help when our foundations are shaking, only to learn that it is God who is shaking them."[18] We should not regard suffering as a strange phenomenon, but rather as a sign of God's work in our lives. Serving through suffering takes a lot of faith and trust, and it makes little sense to look ahead for reasons. For sure, there is a Calvary and a cross for every Christian. Struggle only makes sense after it's over and we look backward.

On a train, some people sit facing forward and some sit facing backward. In leadership, choose to face forward, but every now and then take a glance backward to notice all the things you have already passed. It will give you peace about what might be coming around the next turn.

4
GIFTED
---

t is bizarre that the most capable among us are occasionally the same people who feel inadequate and unaccepted. Many insecure leaders possess a wealth of talent, ability, and gifting, but they are still unsure. This is because our abilities can also be our most significant weaknesses. A person who is at ease when talking within a social circle risks becoming a person who doesn't know when to shut up. An organized person can administrate a project—to death. Musical people often forget that there is more to ministry than singing or playing an instrument.

The more gifted you are, the more likely you are to be dangerous to follow. Gifted people are more likely to neglect spiritual disciplines, struggle with being personally dependant on God, and limit their vision to those things for which they do not need supernatural assistance. In other words, they have a harder time finding their security in God when they can easily find ways to be sure in self.

I am not suggesting that giftedness is wrong, nor am I suggesting that you suppress your gifts. In fact, Scripture tells us to hone them and fan them into flame. But we are also told to keep them in proper perspective. You have probably noticed many gifted people who live only in their areas of skill, to the detriment of the other tasks that need their attention. Those who only live in this safe arena never learn of the security that can only be found in Christ.

Danger #1 – Identity

Based loosely on Robert Ludlum's novel, *The Bourne Identity* is a film about a man whose wounded body is discovered by fishermen who nurse him back to health. He can't remember anything and begins to try to rebuild his memory based on clues. In one scene, Bourne sits in a restaurant struggling to reboot his memory. He has no idea who he is, but he is keenly aware of his innate abilities—he instinctively knows the sight lines in the restaurant, the license plate numbers of every vehicle in the parking lot, and the weight of each restaurant patron. He even knows the most likely place to find a weapon. But none of that information tells him who he is or what he does. Similarly, you cannot look only to the areas in which you are gifted when you are seeking a definition of yourself or a discernment of your ministry role in the Kingdom. Giftedness only provides the clues.

Likewise, you cannot allow a lack of giftedness in a particular area to be the sole reason to exclude yourself from a ministry task. A sovereign God prepares you and makes you ready for the work. As with Moses, who's skillset never matched the task, God's promise ("I will be with you") holds in it the implicit promise of supernatural equipping.

In my case, according to the personality assessment and gift inventories, I have operated outside of my giftedness many times. This only serves to prove the sovereignty of God and the constant supernatural intervention of the Holy Spirit in our lives.

Danger #2 – Approval

Giftedness can be mistaken as God's approval of how we are living our lives. Success and prosperity do not always indicate endorsement, nor do struggle and suffering necessarily point to God's disapproval. There are many gifted people who enjoy tremendous success while their lives are void of integrity.

There are very few formulas in Scripture. We like "if... then" formulas, but they simply don't work. Job walked blamelessly before the Lord and yet endured tremendous hardship. Jacob was blessed, even though deception was his common practice. We want to say that "if" we are experiencing success, "then" God is pleased with our performance. This is simply not always the case. Success does not necessarily mean that God's will has been done. Os Guinness further suggests:

> One of the most common, subtle, and manipulative distortions of all is in religious empire building. God only knows how many churches, missionary societies, charities, colleges, crusades, reforms, and acts of philanthropic generosity have trumpeted the call of God and advanced their leaders' egos. In a generation's time this law will probably be seen as the single greatest problem of the mega-church movement. More than any part of the church of Christ should, today's big churches and parachurch organizations rise and fall by the strength of a single person.[19]

Some ministries have had a lot of success when analyzed with a worldly view, but in the light of eternity they may not have been the desire of God. Thankfully, God has been gracious. In my life, even in the times when I have been "out of God's will," He has used me to minister, but that still did not validate my waywardness. In His kingdom, obedience is always preferred to sacrifice. Doing *some* right things never trumps doing *the* right thing.

Danger #3 – Over-definition

Ministry leaders are often typecast into specific roles, and the Kingdom never gets the full advantage of their more subtle gifts. Giftedness can over-define who you are. This is especially true for those who have public and obvious gifts and skills. Many times, leaders are overlooked because of their primary gifts. If this happens several times, leaders can soon forget to develop other gifts—the ones that are dormant inside them. Time and again I have heard people excuse themselves from personal evangelism or other Kingdom tasks because it's "not their thing." Scripture is clear on what tasks are our "things." Unfortunately, sometimes we use our giftedness to excuse ourselves from God's commands.

Danger #4 – Hardship

Giftedness does not assist us during times of struggle and hardship. Eliphaz, one of Job's first advisors, was quick to point Job to his gifts and accomplishments, but those words offered no comfort. In days of trial, true connection with Christ is the only remaining anchor. In dark times, leaders who have not cultivated closeness with Christ will find that their resources are not sufficient for conquering present struggles. Gifting can never eliminate the insecurity felt in hardship.

Danger #5 – Self-reliance

Worst of all, giftedness can lower our dependence on God. Poor leaders rest on one or two of their primary abilities. Great leaders, however, live just slightly on the other side of their ability. They blaze trails to where their skills alone could not bring them. They see the natural but also consider the supernatural. They live in such a manner that if God doesn't show up, they will fail.

I have had the blessing of being with many gifted people. I have envied (or have been jealous of) their abilities. But when I've been with gifted people who truly have a relationship with Christ, I find myself not only considering their gifts, but challenged by their connection with the Almighty. Each of us has gifts according to the grace given us, but greater than gifts is the presence of Christ in our lives. Gifts are dangerous, unless we have learned to speak with God as a friend speaks with a friend.

Paul summarizes it well in 1 Corinthians 13:

> If I speak in the tongues of men and of angels, but have not love, I am only a resounding gong or a clanging cymbal. If I have the gift of prophecy and can fathom all mysteries and all knowledge, and if I have a faith that can move mountains, but have not love, I am nothing. If I give all I possess to the poor and surrender my body to the flames, but have not love, I gain nothing. (1 Corinthians 13:1–3)

5
SIGHT

I s it really possible to *"live by faith, not by sight"* as 2 Corinthians 5:7 suggests? It has to be! For if we cannot live by faith, it is impossible to live in security, and a leader cannot lead from a place of feeling the acceptance of God.

Honestly, there have been days when I wondered if I could continue to live by a faith that seldom allows me to see what I believe. But without always seeing Him, I believe there is a God, that God made the universe out of nothing, that there is a heaven, and that there is a hell. I accept that there is a Spirit, and that He makes His home in my heart. Blindly I believe that I have been granted forgiveness, but only by the blood of Christ, and because of that I have everlasting life. I do believe that God heals, but not as often as I would like. He miraculously intervenes, but it is not often seen—especially in Canada. I believe He instantly changes people, but many stay the same. I believe God answers when I call out to Him, but it is seldom very loud. However, His love compels me to place my hope in His truths, even when I have doubts.

For a Grade 10 physical education requirement, I joined the high diving class. I thought it would impress girls. The other option would have been to join the volleyball club, and that seemed, well, a little less manly. Truthfully, I had no intention of ever taking the plunge from the high board, because it was acceptable to switch from high diving to volleyball at any time. I could swim well enough, and I could dive from low boards, so I was certain that I could last for several weeks until we moved to the higher boards.

To fully appreciate the dynamics of the situation, you need to know the layout of my high school—a school that also served as our community recreation center. Bleachers on the east side surrounded the swimming pool, and the school cafeteria, with large glass windows, overlooked the pool from the north side.

Day one. I snapped on my swimwear ("trunks" were a little different back then) and made my way to the pool deck with the rest of the class. I was quick to raise my hand when the instructor took a poll to see who already had diving experience. Then came the fateful words of the diving instructor. Words still etched in my mind. Words that still make me shiver: "Jim, you will go first. Let's go to the high diving board."

My plan had failed. My life was over before it ever began. I was certain that the next morning's newspaper would read, "Chubby High School Student Belly-Flops to Death—Pool Closed for Cleaning."

I started to climb the ladder. The air got thinner with each step. Halfway up, I had to stop for a breath from an oxygen tank. People below began to disappear beneath the clouds. Ducks and geese flew by with mocking glances. My stomach was doing flip-flops and my legs were weak, but I reached the top. From there, the pool looked like a meagre puddle.

I was told to walk out to the end of the diving board and wait for instructions. "Sit down on the board and let your legs dangle over the edge," said the cruel instructor, "and put your arms above your head as if you were assuming a diving posture." I was sure that my diving posture would look more like a screaming spread-eagle, but nonetheless I obeyed.

Then, with her many years of instructor training, she offered the next crucial step to making a flawless high-dive. She yelled from below, "Now, simply fall forward off the board." I muttered under my breath. I sat there. I did not fall forward. I was not as dumb as I looked.

"Your body will automatically form into a perfect diving position," she bellowed from below. One position this six-foot, hefty body never forms is a "perfect diving position." A perfect belly-flop position is what this body automatically makes. Perhaps it could even be contorted into a cannonball position, but never a "perfect diving position."

By now a crowd had gathered against the windows of the cafeteria, and some had filled the bleachers. But I did not fall forward. I just sat there. With my arms above my head, I sat there. I continued to sit there for what seemed like hours. The instructor kept urging me to dive ("fall"). Classmates were yelling at me to hurry. But I just froze. I prayed for a fire drill. I prayed for a bomb threat. I even prayed that the coming of Jesus would rapture me out of this situation. Finally, wanting the agony to end, I fell forward. As anticipated, my body formed the perfect belly-flop position. The water turned to concrete. Glass around the cafeteria shattered from the shockwaves of the smack of my flesh hitting the water. I crawled out of the pool, defeated and embarrassed. It was days later before I could successfully remove my shorts.

Sitting on the edge of the diving board, I kept waiting for a better understanding before I took the plunge. People were yelling instructions. The instructor was telling me exactly what would happen. They assured me that many had done this before. But I just sat there, waiting and hoping for some supernatural revelation. The only way I could fully know the experience was to take the plunge for myself. No amount of argument, debate, or persuasion could help me experience that dive. I had to jump in.

You can sit on the edge of faith, waiting for all the questions to be answered, but you will never come to God by debating all the kinks and arguments. You have to let yourself go—into God's love—by faith. You can still find God in the midst of unanswered questions. You just have to accept that you will never have all the answers.

The Bible says a lot of things that I do not understand, and there are so many things that don't make sense in the world. As I write these words, I'm sitting in a coffee shop listening to a mother explain to her wheelchair-bound child that the surgeon will be drilling two holes into the child's head to properly fit a new steel halo. At the table next to me is a man who could not say "hello" to me properly because he does not have the ability to speak or hear.

So I have a lot of questions. But I am sure of my relationship with God. It is not a blind faith. There are lots of evidence and arguments for belief in God. Billions have made a commitment to follow Jesus, but at the end of the day I serve Jesus "in faith."

The Bible says, *"Now we see but a poor reflection as in a mirror; then we shall see face to face. Now I know in part; then I shall know fully, even as I am fully known."* (1 Corinthians 13:12). There are plenty of proofs that God is real and that He loves you, but you will have to accept that **by faith**. I can parade believer after believer in front of you and have them tell of their encounters with God, but you will still have to fall into Him **by faith**. I could tell you about the Cosmological Argument for God's existence that says everything has a cause, and therefore God is the initial "First Cause", but you will still have to choose **by faith**. I could tell you about the Moral Argument—that our sense of moral values points to the existence of a moral Creator—but you'll still need to believe **by faith**. I could talk about the Teleological Argument, that says evidence of design and purpose in the world points to intelligent creation, as a watch indicates a watchmaker, but you will still have to come **in faith**. You might like to hear about the unparalleled reliability and accuracy of the historical text of the Bible, or about the confirmation of the events, places, nations, and people of the Bible by archaeology, but if you want to talk to Jesus it will be **by faith.** If God was small enough to be understood, He wouldn't be big enough to handle your sin.

The Bible says, *"Now faith is being sure of what we hope for and certain of what we do not see."* (Hebrews 11:1). It sounds weird, but you can only be certain by faith. You can stay seated on the edge, or you can fall into God and be certain. The Word says that no one can come to God unless the Spirit of God draws him or her. The tug that people feel inside, in the middle of all the unanswered questions, is the Spirit's drawing. It is the Holy Spirit (think instructor or dive coach) that invites people into that relationship—not the reasoning alone.

Jesus said, *"Because you have seen me, you have believed."* (John 20:29). John 20 also gives us four instances of those who had to see before they could believe. First, it mentions John who comes to faith not by seeing Jesus himself but by seeing the empty burial wrappings. Second, Mary Magdalene sees Jesus but does not recognize and confess Him as Lord until He calls her name. Third, the disciples see Jesus before believing it is really Him. Fourth is Thomas; he also sees Jesus and then believes, but only after insisting on a sign.

When Jesus left the earth and went to the Father in heaven, He left a new kind of faith: a belief without having physical, visible "in the flesh" encounters with the resurrected Christ. He tells us about another kind of faith: *"Blessed are those who have not seen and yet have believed"* (John 20:29). So we must cease being so cerebral. Sure, we must be reasonable and approach faith intellectually, but we cannot neglect the beautiful mystery. It is a wonderful complexity. One of the most conflicting yet profound statements in Scripture is: *"I do believe; help me overcome my unbelief!"* (Mark 9:24).

Across Germany at the end of World War II, Allied forces searched farms and houses looking for snipers. Allegedly, at one abandoned house, searchers with flashlights found their way to the basement. There, on the crumbling wall, a victim of the Holocaust had scratched a Star of David. Beneath it, in rough lettering, was scrawled: "I believe in the sun—even when it does not shine; I believe in love—even when it is not shown; I believe in God—even when He does not speak." These words mirror some of the lyrics of the song *I Believe in Love*, by Barlow Girl:

> How long will my prayers seem unanswered?
> Is there still faith in me to reach the end?
> I'm feeling doubt, I'm losing faith
> But giving up would cost me everything
> So I'll stand in the pain and silence
> And I'll speak to the dark night
>
> I believe in the sun even when it's not shining
> I believe in love even when I don't feel it
> And I believe in God even when He is silent
> And I, I believe
>
> Though I can't see my stories ending
> That doesn't mean the dark night has no end
> It's only here that I find faith
> And learn to trust the one who writes my days
> So I'll stand in the pain and silence
> And I'll speak to the dark night[20]

I am "silly" enough to believe in everything the Word claims. I am not clever enough to figure it all out, so *"though [I] have not seen him, [I] love him; and even though [I] do not see him now, [I] believe in him and [am] filled with an inexpressible and glorious joy, for [I am] receiving the goal of [my] faith, the salvation of [my soul]"* (1 Peter 1:8–9).

This is foolishness to those who are perishing, but to me who is being saved it is the power of God (1 Corinthians 1:18). In the times when God seems quiet, I know it is only for a season. There will be a demonstration of the Spirit's power. Rick Warren once tweeted, "God gave NO answer to Job's pain for 39 chapters! Only silence! Trials test my faith by not knowing how far I am from Chapter 40!"[21]

I know my sons live in security because of the way they respond to me. They are still small enough to think that Daddy will never let them down. They still leap off furniture knowing I will catch them. (In fact, they usually don't even wait to see if I'm ready to grab them.)

So take the plunge. It'll be okay. The enemy of our faith is not unbelief—it's pride. The old adage is still sound advice, "Let go, and let God."

6

BITTER

One of Sandy's favourite movies is *The Princess Bride*. In it is a character named Inigo Montoya who spends most of his life searching for the man who killed his father. He constantly rehearses the words he will use when he finds his father's killer: "My name is Inigo Montoya. You killed my father. Prepare to die."

When he finally finds the killer and avenges his father's death, he is asked what he will do now that he has gotten his revenge. Inigo has a puzzled look on his face and then says, "Is very strange. I have been in the revenge business so long, now that it's over, I don't know what to do with the rest of my life."

If leaders remain in leadership long enough, unresolved issues in their heart, like bitterness and jealousy, will emerge into the forefront of their leadership life. Bitterness becomes a scab that enemies will pick at until it bleeds again.

Our tendency is to see our bitterness as a statement about someone else, but it is actually a commentary about ourselves. I know about bitterness, and so do you. It is a temptation every person experiences. Proverbs 14:10 says, *"Each heart knows its own bitterness."* James 3:14–16 adds, *"But if you harbor bitter envy and selfish ambition in your hearts, do not boast about it or deny the truth. Such 'wisdom' does not come down from heaven but is earthly, unspiritual, of the devil. For where you have envy and selfish ambition, there you find disorder and every evil practice."* It is impossible to be secure and bitter at the same time.

There are some bitter people in leadership. Their motto is: if life gives you lemons, throw them at someone! There are aggravations and annoyances in this noble calling, so bitter people usually feel they have good reason. But reasons cannot be allowed to be excuses. Bitterness is a sin, not an emotion. In fact, in Ephesians it is listed among sins like *"rage and anger, brawling and slander, along with every form of malice."* (Ephesians 4:31).

Bitterness is not a state, condition, or rite of passage granted to those who are hard done by. Bitterness is wrong, harms our physical health, strains our relationships, and dampens our spiritual journey. It must be overcome or else we will drown. It is not what happens to us that will sink our boat; a ship only sinks when what is on the outside gets into the inside. It is only what we allow to enter our heart that will reap destruction.

Because bitterness is a sin, it can be enjoyable. It is sort of like being glum and finding a slow sad song to make us feel better by making us feel worse. Thankfully, those feelings usually pass. But every so often they take root, and since each of us has failings and shortcomings we tend to blame our bitterness on the external conditions imposed on us. We wrestle with feelings of entitlement and martyrdom, especially in seasons of inconvenience, lack of appreciation, or personal infringement. We become upset or withdrawn when things do not go our way. Whenever we believe that *our* difficult circumstance is clearly an exception, resentment festers into bitterness. This will kill us, softly, without us really being aware of what is happening.

Several years ago, I watched a famous talk show host interview the former employee of a company that had treated him unfairly. It seemed his point was valid and, indeed, he had been a victim. The employee barked, "I will hate that company until the day I die." Capping the interview, the wise interviewer responded, "I wonder who that will hurt more—you or the company?" Forgetting what is behind and reaching forward to what is ahead is seldom easy, but it may help to be reminded of these four things:

1. It is not always the ministry's fault. Indeed, there are peculiar paradigms for pastors. We serve the ones we lead. Life and ministry are blended. Our spiritual journey is public and under the microscope. We have to do what we say, and apologize earnestly if we don't. But those are not always the reasons for our struggles. We must not blame the ministry for every situation that makes life challenging. More often, the bad days come simply because we are alive.

2. Be not wary only the fierce wolf, but the pestering Chihuahua! A friend of ours has a Chihuahua named "Chippy." Chippy is only a couple of pounds. Compared to a wolf, Chippy is no threat at all, but his incessant yapping can send the strongest man over the edge!

There are strong attacks from large enemies. Nonetheless, we are not usually destroyed by the chomp of a shark, but by the incessant nibbling of tiny piranhas. So yes, sweat the small stuff and keep it in perspective, avoiding the temptation to make things larger than they are.

3. Our heart condition is more important than our circumstance. If we spent as much time mastering the right attitude as we do mastering the right techniques, we would be champions. Bitterness is sneaky. *"Above all else, guard your heart, for it is the wellspring of life."* (Proverbs 4:23). It takes a lot of effort to maintain a healthy heart. We shape our inner lives by the way we choose to think about our circumstances. So, in many ways, our emotions are a choice. We behave the way we do because we think the way we do.

4. Delete the file. Hurts and hassles are often stored close by so that they are available for easy recall. Let them go. Erase the chalkboard. Clear the scoreboard. Love keeps no record of wrongs. Thank God that we can have frequent and meaningful new beginnings. Forgiveness is choosing to live with the consequences of someone else's behaviour. Even if other people believe mistruths about us, we must learn to be willing to live with the tarnish.

Here's an imagination exercise for you. Hebrews 12:15 says, *"See to it that no one misses the grace of God and that no **bitter root** grows up to cause trouble and defile many."* (emphasis added). So if there exists *"bitter roots,"* what does the tree look like? What kind of fruit hangs off its branches?

7
SYMPTOMS

After enduring feelings of hopelessness and despair, a man finally decided to seek the aid of a psychologist. He lay on the couch, painfully spilled his emotions, and then waited for the profound wisdom of the psychologist to make him feel better. The doctor asked him a few more questions, then wrote furiously in his notebook while the man sat in silence for what seemed like hours. Suddenly, the psychologist looked up and pronounced his diagnosis. "Your problem is low self-esteem," the doctor explained. "It is very common among losers."

• • •

Symptoms are always clues to a greater problem. Symptoms are not the disease and will always be present unless the systemic condition is resolved. The disease might still be present even if the symptoms are medicated or masked.

In 2003, I bought a new Volkswagen Jetta. It has become like a member of the family. Seven years and 350,000 kilometres later, we still don't have the heart (read "money") to part with it. Within a week of buying it, I was nicely settled in to a long drive when suddenly I was jolted into attention by an ungodly beeping sound. I discovered that the fuel tank was getting low and a warning light had illuminated on the console. If you have never heard the piercing warning tone of a Jetta, you've missed a powerful experience. The volume is shocking. However, these days I hardly notice when the warning chimes. (Yet it's still fun watching my passengers jump.)

Our lives have warning tones and, unfortunately, we can become adept at tuning them out. Some of these signs are guilt, fear, despair, tiredness, anxiety, poor health, and depression. If we ignore them, they will be silenced, but only until a real problem develops. It is too late to address the warnings when you're stranded on the roadside of leadership watching others pass you by.

Writing a book about insecurity has brought many amusing comments from friends. Most often, they uneasily ask one ironic question: "A book on insecurity? Am I in it?" (I usually tell them that a whole chapter has been dedicated to them.) We are a pretty fragile bunch, aren't we? Scores of leaders are scared and full of self-doubt.

To illustrate some of the "symptoms," here are a few people (identities concealed) I have met along the way. Perhaps you will see some of these markers of insecurity in your own life. For me, each of these insecurities existed in my life in varied intensities and in various seasons. Many of them are primarily manifested during times of conflict or stress, causing insecure leaders to make surprisingly unwise, risky, and bizarre decisions. Insecurity and leadership make for a volatile concoction.

Flawless Frank

When I met Frank, he struck me as confident, fun, and friendly. I liked him. I like him still. Few people are as genuinely caring and willing to offer to help another person. Frank was involved, purposeful, and proactive in local church ministry and a faithful witness to everyone in his life. In every task, he was reliable and responsible.

Frank obsessed about doing everything with high excellence and he expected no less of everyone else—especially those under his leadership, as well as in his family. Yet, two of his daughters no longer serve the Lord. In fact, their behaviour bears little resemblance to Christian character.

It didn't take too long to notice that Frank was quick to correct others and proud to tell of how he heavy-handed someone or "rebuked" him or her. Frank was swift to let everyone know about his disciplined life and high moral standards. But Frank had a secret sin, one that he did not know I was aware of. Many of the times when he pointed out the sin of other people, it would be the same sin in which he was involved. Frank had set up a tribunal of his own making and presided over others. While seeming impeccably disciplined and consistent in his life's externals, the internals were not as well-managed. He did ministry well, but was poor at doing life.

Strangely, perfectionists like Frank often consider themselves superior to others, yet at the same time they are fully alert to their own imperfections—imperfections they are frequently able to rationalize or justify. Thus, their feelings toggle between deficiency and pride.

Not every "perfectionist" is as judgmental as Frank. Nor do they all appear as confident and self-assured. Some perfectionists are more timid and "seem very insecure, doubting their decisions and actions, fearing mistakes and rejection, and having low opinions of themselves; at the same time, they have excessively high personal standards and an exaggerated emphasis on precision, order and organization, which suggests aspiration to be better than others."[22] It would be fair to say that Frank was a "high achiever," an overachiever, yet he always felt as though he was one more task away from success. Wherever there is an overachiever, there is an underachiever close by. Others nearby will not accept responsibility or try to succeed for themselves. If the overachiever is a leader, followers are more than happy to let the leader do all the work.

No one in Frank's life or ministry was permitted to share Frank's tasks. He would often complain of not having anyone to carry the load with him. Truth be told, however, Frank did not want anyone else to taint the project by not doing it the way he wanted it done. For him, "good enough" was never good enough. He could be heard saying, "If you want something done right, you have to do it yourself." Perfectionism's twin is "control." The perfectionist gains a sense of control, comfort, and safety when things he is responsible for are close to perfect.

Frank had a need to criticize others' work, while constantly blaming external factors when his own work was subpar. In his mind, perfection was never attained because an interruption came along, or someone did a sloppy job, or there were just too many other pressures to allow him to do things right. You could get away with insulting Frank personally more than you could get away with insulting his work.

When perfectionism approaches a severe level, it can be considered dysfunctional and compulsive. For the perfectionist, "want to" becomes "have to" in work and in life.

Perfectionists, when driven by insecurity, determine that if anything has the chance of reflecting poorly on them, they are compelled to log a record of the blame. There is a need to create "escape hatches" by making sure everyone knows that a project is only a "rough draft" or adding qualifiers to any presented work. They are unable to delineate between perfectionism and excellence. Their interpretation of others' behaviour and their analyses of situations are never completely plumb with reality.

Psychiatrist Dr. David Burns, an expert on the subject of perfectionism, writes:

> I do not mean the healthy pursuit of excellence by men and women who take genuine pleasure in striving to meet high standards. Without concern for quality, life would seem shallow; true accomplishment would be rare. The perfectionists I am talking about are those whose standards are high beyond reach or reason, people who strain compulsively and unremittingly toward impossible goals and who measure their self-worth entirely in terms of productivity and accomplishment.[23]

Not every perfectionist is highly insecure, but when they are they resist change, tending to stay in their comfort zones.

Performance Pete

Pete's ministry years were spent mining for compliments in the sandbox of leadership achievement in order to find his security. After many seasons of giving intense, high-achieving, and successful leadership, Pete crashed. It took several years for this approval addict to regain the confidence to begin serving in leadership again.

Like all performers, Pete had a paralyzing fear of failure. He became dejected when he failed. He was critical of himself and was a self-help addict. Worry and anxiety turned into full-blown panic and anxiety attacks. I must add, what you fear reveals what you value the most and what you fear reveals where you trust God the least.

Performers live reactionary lifestyles (as opposed to "strategic" or "intentional" ones). They think that satisfaction and contentment are only one work task away. They are good at solving everyone's problems except their own, intoxicating themselves with work so they do not have to face their personal reality. Their workloads are huge. They need to keep everyone happy. Burnout and sickness is their destiny. They are often conflict avoiders, preferring to cover things up rather than deal with them. An insecure "performer" is easily swayed by public opinion, lacks discipline, and resists being corrected or taught.

In his book, *The Search for Significance*, Robert McGee pointedly writes:

> Unfortunately, many of us give only lip service to the powerful truths of the Scriptures without allowing them to affect the basis of our self-esteem in a radical way. Instead, we continue to seek our security and purpose from worldly sources: personal success, status, beauty, wealth, and the approval of others. These rewards may fulfill us for a short time, but they soon lead us to a sense of urgency to succeed and the need to be approved of again.[24]

Like all performers, Pete's subconscious belief was, "I must meet certain standards to feel good about myself." He was scared of hurting other people's feelings. He would rather be hurt than hurt someone else. He feared losing approval. He had a hard time saying "no."

After several years of successful ministry, my friend and colleague Brad left formal ministry to prepare to become a physician. His long-term goal was to become a medical missionary. Now that he is fully immersed in the medical world, our chats are insightful. The parallels between medical leadership and ministry leadership are remarkable. Doctors are experiencing burnout at the same rate as ministry leaders. As with pastoring, there is always one more call they can make. Every time they decide to engage in self-care, a patient is getting less care. Some are overdriven and predisposed to it for a plethora of reasons. The motivation is prestige or money for some, while for others there exists a strong desire to help the suffering and make a real difference for humanity. And still others are fuelled by insecurity.

Leader, do not ignore the signals of your own exhaustion or discouragement. Your spiritual health is directly proportional to the speed and pace of your life. If you are too busy, you have an approval addiction. You want to appear important. The truth is that being "too busy" should not be a flattering term. It should illuminate caution signs telling you that you are running ahead of the will of God for your life. Having people tell you that you are too busy shouldn't be taken as a compliment. Busyness is a value of a performance-addicted person.

Paranoid Paula

Beth Moore writes of paranoid leaders, "Insecurity lives in constant terror of loss. Insecure people are always afraid that something or somebody is going to be taken from them."[25]

I have witnessed this dynamic even in my own children. Our middle son, Ethan, is exceptionally personable and wears his emotions outwardly. When Brody, our youngest, was a newborn I was playing on the floor with him while Ethan stood at my side. Without warning, Ethan sunk his little teeth into my shoulder. I yelped! Ethan went silent. Brody screeched. Sandy came running into the room.

In Ethan's limited communicative ability, he struggled to find a way to express his fear that this new addition would cause him to lose the attention and favour he was accustomed to. Now, a few years later, these brothers are constant companions and inseparable friends. In the early morning, whichever one wakes first immediately wakes the other so that they can begin another day of destruction. But in the newborn days, Ethan could not see the gift he was receiving and only observed the threat of loss.

Paranoid Paula was a grown-up version of Ethan. Any prospect of loss would trigger her insecurity. She had no reason to be paranoid. She was liked and admired. People sought her counsel often. She held a high position with a ministry organization and, although she did not believe it, she was highly favoured. But Paula's insecurity filled her with thoughts and fears of losing her position. Her worth was complexly entangled with the leadership post she held.

I learned quickly that when Paula asked for my opinion or critique, she did not really want to hear my response unless it was positive. She was suspicious of people (causing isolation) and distrusted institutions and authority. Paula always had a concealed agenda and assumed that others had similar intentions. For her, everyone had an ulterior motive.

Paranoid leaders are afraid of real things, and sometimes of things imagined. They cannot enjoy people and do not get too close to others. They question everyone's motives. They always feel like a rebellion is in the works. They do not like criticism and overreact to it. They are jealous of talented people, especially their staff or colleagues. A paranoid leader is unable to hire someone better at something than he or she is. Paranoid, insecure leaders blame situations and institutions for their own faults. They can be "anti-establishment," mocking the authority structure and blaming the system.

On one occasion, Paula was chatting with me about the intense workload and high expectations placed on her. I suggested that she delegate a particular job function to her colleague who was quite competent in that area. I was surprised at her abrupt response. "I can't let Chris do that! The person who does that will be the person who replaces me!"

Paula's fear reminds me of the paranoia in my own life. For me, it is a daily decision to leave the politics to God and rest in the reality that God is in control. I will not allow myself to feel threatened or consider the need to guard my position or power.

When insecurity breeds paranoia, the outcome is withdrawal. This means the avoidance of failure and risk. Furthermore, the only close relationships permitted are with people who give esteem-building attention and relate to the leader therapeutically. People who struggle with this type of insecurity are often alcoholics, extremely defensive, lack self-control, live in isolation, or engage in other sinful behaviour. Insecurity puts them in lockdown. There are places they will not go and people they will not see because they are scared of what people might think, say, or do.

Blamer Bill

The most insecure person I have ever met was Pastor Bill. Another pastor decided to plant a church in the same town as Bill's church. Bill exploded with a storm of accusations and arguments.

Oddly, Bill's church had created some unique ministries that were going well and these new strategies were bringing new people into the church. In fact, some of the ministries created in the church were unlike any I had seen before. He had no reason to be bothered. He was consistently taking new ground until the new "threat" began to eat away at his spirit.

It seemed that he was continuously creating escape routes for his pride. He blamed people. He blamed his colleagues. He blamed the leaders above him and below him. There was always a plan to save face if projects went belly-up. A disclaimer accompanied every effort. If it were a sermon, he would start by highlighting his head cold. If it were an outreach event, he would note the poor weather or a neighbouring church's event. If you were a guest in his church, you were told, "Our numbers are down today because [insert excuse here]."

Blamers use the word "if" a lot. "If only I received the same special treatment as that leader." Or, "If I had that opportunity, I would have been able to accomplish the same thing." Or, "If that leader would stop sabotaging me, I would have a chance to get ahead."

What's unique about Blamers is that they usually have an uncanny ability to create a culture of blame within their organization. Their followers drink the same poison, learning to ignore their own shortcomings and pick up the same offenses and conflicts as their leader.

Blamers are addicted to comparison. Women, in particular, are really good at insecurity-rooted comparison. In Moore's survey of more than 900 women, it was found that 78% admitted to having feelings of insecurity at or above a level that bothers them. 43% described their issues with insecurity as anywhere from "pretty big" to "huge."

Beth Moore continues, "Our constant propensity to compare ourselves to the women around us is wrecking our perceptions of both ourselves and them. Most of us are not in a public place for five minutes before we peruse the female players in the room and judge where we rank."[26] Of course, men do likewise. I often have to remind myself of Galatians 5:26—"We [must] not compare ourselves with each other as if one of us were better and another worse." (The Message)

Connor the Controller

Controllers are insecure people who produce an environment where insecurities abound. They create a draining and exhausting environment. The people around them are confused and nervous because they never know what is going to happen next.

Control is always a symptom of insecurity or psychosis (or both). The amount of control the insecure person exerts is directly proportional to the perceived threat of another individual's skill, talent, charisma, or spiritual maturity. Control is linked powerfully to pride. To some degree, every leader has a control problem because every leader has a pride problem. Terry Cooper writes, "If I search around long enough, I'll find insecurity beneath my grandiosity and arrogant expectations beneath my self-contempt."[27] Pride leads to arrogance, arrogance to pompous aspirations, then to self-destruction.

A friend told me about Connor the Controller, an upper-level leader who spent time searching for skeletons in the closets of other leaders. He had special access to a few websites that gave him information about people's current situation and history. He once attempted to launch a formal investigation from information he found out about a ministry leader, even though the information was only a minor offense.

Connor had a file on everyone. He would remind people about it. "Your file is sure getting thick!" he would quip. He kept a record of his colleagues' failures—especially subordinates. His insecurity repeatedly made talented and gifted friends into enemies and competitors. Make no mistake; insecurity looks a lot like jealousy, and serving in leadership always amplifies jealousy. Robert A. Heinlein, in his novel *Time Enough for Love*, says, "A competent and self-confident person is incapable of jealousy in anything. Jealousy is invariably a symptom of neurotic insecurity."[28] Are you a controller? Here are a few questions to ask:

Do you give credit to others?

Do you have positive hopes for your successor?

Do you handle heroes and champions well?

Are you free from an unhealthy need to feel highly important, essential, and irreplaceable in the organization?

Are you free from feeling the compulsion to maintain absolute order?

Are you able to easily separate your work from your personal life?

Do you not withhold information from people? Max DePree said, "The right to know is basic. Moreover, it is better to err on the side of sharing too much information than risk leaving someone in the dark. Information is power, but it is pointless power if hoarded. Power must be shared for an organization or a relationship to work."[29]

Is delegating easy for you? Do you empower people? Are you quick to give permission?

Can you hire someone more gifted than yourself? Can you hire to your weakness?

Moses felt he had to be in control. The following account from Exodus 18 provides some wise counsel for controllers:

> The next day Moses took his place to judge the people. People were standing before him all day long, from morning to night. When Moses' father-in-law saw all that he was doing for the people, he said, "What's going on here? Why are you doing all this, and all by yourself, letting everybody line up before you from morning to night?"
>
> Moses said to his father-in-law, "Because the people come to me with questions about God. When something comes up, they come to me. I judge between a man and his neighbour and teach them God's laws and instructions."
>
> Moses' father-in-law said, "This is no way to go about it. You'll burn out, and the people right along with you. This is way too much for you—you can't do this alone. Now listen to me. Let me tell you how to do this so that God will be in this with you. Be there for the people before God, but let the matters of concern be presented to God. Your job is to teach them the rules and instructions, to show them how to live, what to do. And then you need to keep a sharp eye out for competent men—men who fear God, men of integrity, men who are incorruptible—and appoint them as leaders over groups organized by the thousand, by the hundred, by fifty, and by ten. They'll be responsible for the everyday work of judging among the people. They'll bring the hard cases to you, but in the routine cases they'll be the judges. They will share your load and that will make it easier for you. If you handle the work this way, you'll have the strength to carry out whatever God commands you, and the people in their settings will flourish also."
>
> Moses listened to the counsel of his father-in-law and did everything he said. Moses picked competent men from all Israel and set them as leaders over the people who were organized by the thousand, by the hundred, by fifty, and by ten. They took over the everyday work of judging among the people. They brought the hard cases to Moses, but in the routine cases they were the judges. Then Moses said good-bye to his father-in-law who went home to his own country. (Exodus 18:13–27, The Message)

Hmmm… I wonder if a controller has a dangerously perfect blend of insecurity and arrogance?

There are times when, as a leader, we want to clean, polish, and control. We want it all to be tidy and "in order." But life, especially life in community, is just not that simple. Trying to control everything is about as effective as trying to nail Jell-O to a wall. Our desire for structure and formula is often met by fluidity and subjectivity. We can drive ourselves into insanity and insecurity if we have to have everything "just so." We avoid being generous or grace-giving because we are scared of creating a precedent that might bind us. We are afraid to deal with one person, so we write a policy for all. We try to manage people by rules rather than relationship.

I must mention the Controller's twin brother—the bully. Who is more afraid, the bullied or the bully? It is the bully who lives in insecurity. The last gasp of an insecure person is to lash out. The bully fakes confidence. He needs to be in control. He is driven by fear, not by the power he pretends to have. Some leaders are so cocksure that they alone have God's plan for their church or organization that when others challenge that plan, they are pegged as evil, contrary, or unspiritual. They are labeled as troublemakers. They are bullied into silence.

God wants leaders to lead in truth, not power. The godly leader never confronts power with power, but confronts power with truth, and always in love.

Larry the Liar

A preacher once concluded his service by saying, "Next Sunday I am going to preach on the subject of lying. In preparation for the message, I would like you all to read Mark 17. By a show of hands, who promises to read the text?" Almost all the hands raised.

The following Sunday, the preacher said, "Now, all of you who have done as I requested and read Mark 17, please raise your hands."

Nearly every hand in the congregation went up.

The preacher continued, "Perfect. You are the people I want to talk to. There is no Mark 17."

The human psyche is full of defence mechanisms. One of them is our propensity to lie. The phone rings and the call awakens us.

"Sorry, were you sleeping? Did I wake you?" the voice on the other end asks.

"Oh. No. I was just sitting on the sofa," we respond. We would hate for anyone to think we take naps.

When someone offers us a second helping of dinner, we say, "No, I'm full, thank you." The truth is, we don't want to appear like a glutton.

When someone asks us for a favour, we say, "Really, it's no trouble." But honestly, we'd rather watch television.

When our wife asks us to take out the garbage, we say, "Garbage? Yep. I was just on my way to put that out, sweetie." After all, a happy wife means a happy life.

I did not know Larry well, but he felt the need to "bulk up" his resume with little stories of his own making. He never felt as competent and/or worthy as those around him, so he embellished. Lying is a common symptom of insecurity. (This is different from exaggeration, especially the bragging kind.) Larry would tell us how he could have been a wealthy businessman, but he chose the ministry. On one occasion, as a twenty-year-old, he was offered a job in the tech department of a mining company with a salary of $80,000 per year. (He turned it down.) A professional sports team also scouted him. (Turns out he only played in a game when a scout was visiting.)

Lying is the inclination of all insecure people. They make up stories to explain their circumstance and validate the roadblocks that have stopped them. They lie about a conscious decision they once made that now proves their current reality is present by choice, not chance. They lie when they fail. They lie when they succeed. They lie when they feel inadequate. They lie when there is a risk of not being liked.

As a child, I once called my friend Kevin over to my backyard to finally let him in on a secret I had held from him. Sitting him down, I informed him that I was actually adopted by my parents and was from another planet from a neighbouring galaxy. Furthermore, I possessed many peculiar abilities and supernatural powers. Kevin's quick response was, "Me too!" (Only he was able to name the planet!) That settled, we left the yard to save the world.

Why do we insist on fabricating stories to validate our unique worth?

Self-Focused Sheila

Sheila got angry with me. After several sessions of rehashing the same concerns and issues, I finally said, "Sheila, I am concerned about you and want your life to be abundant, but I am finished meeting with you. You don't want to work on your issues. You just enjoy the attention that your issues bring!"

Some sick people would be absolutely miserable if God healed their illness. They cherish their infirmity so much that they wouldn't know what to do without it! When insecurity is severe, everything revolves around self. These types of people are often very negative about themselves and everything else. They put others down to make themselves look better. They do not invigorate or hearten the people around them; they tend to drain and exhaust them.

I am sure you have a Sheila in your life. She has a pessimistic outlook. She feels that she has no support. She has emotional outbursts that do not relate to the topic at hand and are out of place or exaggerated. She is stubborn. Often she tries to gain control by appearing sad, angry, or withdrawn. She loves for people to ask if she is okay. She finds it difficult to celebrate other people's success. Oddly, Sheila fears achievement because of what it might require of her.

Moses is another example of this sort of narcissism. Moses had a number of traits similar to Self-Focused Sheila. Despite the obvious manipulative presence of God throughout his upbringing, and although he shared in spectacular encounters with Him, Moses still felt captive to his past. Even after seeing "burning bushes," Moses was obsessed with his own inadequacy. He doubted people would follow his God-appointed lead. He could not stop seeing himself as the make or break factor in the fulfillment of God's plan, and when Moses asked the self-focused "am I?" questions, God responded with a profound, "I am." Insecure people often ask "am I" questions. "Am I smart?" "Am I good-looking?" "Am I good enough?" "Am I liked?" "Am I capable?"

King Saul: A Catalogue of Insecurity Symptoms

Saul was rejected by God and full of pride, selfishness, and insecurity. He was self-deceived, had low self-worth, and was extremely paranoid. Scripture says he was handsome, talented, and gifted.

As an insecure leader, he was prone to shifting blame and took no responsibility for actions or omissions. In 1 Samuel 15, he is caught disobeying the Lord's specific command. He blames the soldiers. When Samuel pushes him, Saul gives a half-hearted apology, but still blames the people. Scripture records the rest of the story:

Whatever Saul sent him to do, David did it so successfully that Saul gave him a high rank in the army. This pleased all the people, and Saul's officers as well.

When the men were returning home after David had killed the Philistine, the women came out from all the towns of Israel to meet King Saul with singing and dancing, with joyful songs and with tambourines and lutes.

As they danced, they sang: "Saul has slain his thousands, and David his tens of thousands."

Saul was very angry; this refrain galled him. "They have credited David with tens of thousands," he thought, "but me with only thousands. What more can he get but the kingdom?" And from that time on Saul kept a jealous eye on David.

The next day an evil spirit from God came forcefully upon Saul. He was prophesying in his house, while David was playing the harp, as he usually did. Saul had a spear in his hand and he hurled it, saying to himself, "I'll pin David to the wall." But David eluded him twice.

Saul was afraid of David, because the Lord was with David but had left Saul. So he sent David away from him and gave him command over a thousand men, and David led the troops in their campaigns. In everything he did he had great success, because the Lord was with him. When Saul saw how successful he was, he was afraid of him. (1 Samuel 18:5-15)

Saul was the epitome of a paranoid leader living in constant suspicion. He was wary of Samuel and distrustful of David. On one occasion, Saul became enraged by David's leadership success, even though Saul was a key reason for David's rise in leadership.

As an approval addict, Saul feared people more than God. He was self-seeking, self-focused, and jealous. He lived in crippling fear. His insecurity drove him into leadership that was destructive to others. Even those who were his friends soon became a threat.

8

ARROGANT

Is every arrogant person an insecure person?

The psychology of arrogance is quite complicated and professionals are divided about the connection between arrogance and insecurity. After researching the debate, I feel most comfortable asserting that arrogance is always due to insecurity. Arrogance is insecurity's masquerade. However, the interpretation of the nature of arrogance is extremely subjective, especially across different cultures and socio-economic strata.

One can easily view a person's arrogance as confidence, or vice versa. Arrogant people typically have an inflated sense of self-importance that masks deeper feelings of inadequacy. Power hides fear. They can even develop the skill of speaking about themselves humbly while acting with great arrogance.

Arrogance is a defence mechanism for when a person is feeling vulnerable. This is occasionally learned in childhood when a parent or family member regularly disapproves of a child—usually for not being good enough or for being weak in several areas. Into adulthood, that child assumes the psychological posture of being unworthy or inept. They create arrogance as self-defence. It may shield them briefly, but soon everyone sees the facade. If you are arrogant, everyone knows it. Most are just too gracious to tell you.

There is enormous dissimilarity between a big ego and a strong ego. For example, a "strong" ego is resilient while the "big" ego is frail. The strong, confident leader can handle failure, while the large-ego leader crumbles and gets disheartened easily, and for longer periods of time. The bigger the ego, the weaker the ego. In other words, the inflated ego is more susceptible to deflation by life's pricks. Inflation is always the exaggeration of substance.

To answer the "arrogant or confident" question, we must analyze the traits of each. I would suggest that the "big" ego people are less secure. Of course, no one person is exclusively either. Here is a breakdown of some of the traits:

"Big" Ego	"Strong" Ego
Falls harder, more disheartened	More effective at rebounding
Easily upset at others and self	Has a large capacity for calm
Rigid	Flexible, adaptable
Reactive, lashes out	Stable, employs cognitive tools
Resists criticism or feedback	Looks for the truth in criticism
Fakes self-confidence	Is self-confident
Ignores or avoids reality	Is realistic, uses fair estimates
Dogmatic or "know it all"	Other's viewpoints are welcomed
Seeks inflation by others	Seeks to encourage and help others
Self-preoccupation	Preoccupied with people and tasks
Show-off, attracts attention	Feels less need for external validation
Has to be right	Knows when to yield rights
Employs disguise and pretence	Prefers authenticity over image
Competitive	Cooperative
Jealous	Inclined to direct attention toward others
Is a bully	Is a defender of victims

Great people make others feel great. Small people make others feel small. Insecurity itself can be dangerous in leadership, but insecurity plus arrogance is a precarious potion of the worst parts of our psyche mixed with the power to influence and affect others.

In his book, *Good to Great*, Jim Collins identifies humility and modesty as the central qualities that allow one to achieve greatness in business. The same truth applies to all institutions, including leadership, marriage, and ministry. Without humility one cannot express gratitude, appreciation, or sympathy for others. A secure leader is a person who takes a little more than his share of the blame and a little less than his share of the credit.

Avoiding arrogance is a vital lesson for mouldable young leaders to discover. This must occur while they are still maturing and in the process of defining themselves and their leadership techniques. If not, they will become self-aggrandized both by their pathway to leadership and the praise they receive along the way. For if we venerate someone into "kingship," he or she will undoubtedly begin to act like royalty and treat everyone else as a mere peasant.

So, are you arrogant and also insecure? Here are a few of questions to ask yourself:

Are you a conversation dominator? Arrogant people usually "don't give two hoots" (as my mother would say) about what other people think, so they do not listen when others talk, and they constantly interrupt. I once spent an hour with a man who, for every story I told and every statement I made, added a better story or refuted my statement. It was annoying. It felt like he was constantly fighting for airtime!

Do you brag? Braggarts feel the compulsion to let people know about their money, recent expensive purchases, travel exploits, or good fortune. The things they show off are endless. Their favourite sound is the tooting of their own horn.

Are you always the victim? Often braggarts feel the need to sensationalize their plights. They talk too much about their problems and misfortunes in order to show their unique ability to overcome obstacles or provide an excuse for any area in which they feel subpar.

Do you feel the need to mock or tease anyone in your presence who appears successful? I know a man who turns into a complete jerk when he is near someone of power or influence. He spends the entire time trying to pull them down. The guest is always dumbfounded at the rudeness and undeserved personal attacks. The braggart will ask awkward questions, provide uncomfortable humour, and declare open season on any tiny flaw the guest may possess.

Do you make fun of people? This comes from an innate need to look better than someone else. Every person has that desire, but confident people suppress it. Arrogant people will openly judge and condemn. They get away with their comments by camouflaging it with joking and teasing. Their proclivity to put others down is unrestrained.

Is it "my way or the highway?" No matter what anyone says or does, egotists will impose their ideas on everyone else. Their understanding of open discussion is artificial. They forget that there is a difference between telling people what *they* think and what *to* think.

Arrogance closes doors on relationships, careers, and leadership proficiency. The very thing braggarts try to avoid is what they reap. They lose respect and credibility. They are tagged as exaggerators or liars. They appear incompetent in their professional lives and unstable in attitude. Here are a few other outcomes of being arrogant:

1. If they tend to be dictators, colleagues give up trying to work with them.
2. Others refuse to give them the information they never tell them the truth in the hope that the egotist will fail.
3. They eventually get ignored and have to move on to new social or professional circles.
4. People will disappoint them because the braggart's demands are ignored. Followers will pretend to be obedient, but the braggart's authority will be subverted.

Helping arrogant people is difficult, but do your best to address their arrogance in a frank, sincere manner. It is best to try to depersonalize it by focusing on what their arrogance might mean for their career or relationships.

Realizing that arrogant people are in fact insecure helps us work with them more effectively. We understand that debating with them is pointless. Applying force against them just accelerates their domineering side. Patience and self-control are always key methods to dealing with the arrogant, yet you must not allow them to attack your esteem or self-worth in return.

If you are often accused of being arrogant, you should seek the help of a counsellor or pastor. This will help you to determine the roots of your insecurity and resulting arrogance.

9
CO-DEPENDENT

"I have the show because I'm insecure. It's my insecurity that makes me want to be a comic, that makes me need the audience."

(Ray Romano)

Do you need leadership or does leadership need you?

Just as some people are addicted to alcohol, drugs, or gambling, there are people, often leaders, who are addicted to solving other people's problems. Caring professions—like pastors, social workers, and counsellors—are fertile for those who need others to help them ascertain their sense of identity. Solving a person's problem (or attempting to) can feel good and validating. This reward is then sought over and over. People love to bring their problems to the leader. Leaders love to solve them. Often the "client" is pleased to bring forward a new problem because they know subconsciously they are meeting the needs of the caregiving person. Thus, a co-dependent leader always has an overloaded schedule—and is proud of it. Unfortunately, too many co-dependents end up in leadership before dealing with their issues.

To clarify, it is perfectly acceptable to feel great about helping someone, but it crosses the line when we feel the need to help somebody in order to be esteemed. Then it becomes a dysfunction, which can progress to an addiction. Co-dependency, then, is a relationship addiction in which one person caring for another person with a substance abuse problem (for example) hinders their recovery by enabling or allowing that person to carry on with their addiction or issue in order to satisfy their (the co-dependant's) own need.

People who are co-dependent often suffer from low self-esteem and feel victimized. They use other people as their main source of fulfillment and happiness. This makes them do for clients what clients should be doing for themselves. The inherent danger is that the client gets worse. To add to that, the co-dependent leader lives subconsciously in fear that the client will leave them; when they do, rejection and loneliness levels begin to spike. Sometimes the insecure co-dependent leader is so reliant upon crisis that it essentially becomes their driving force. If they don't have a crisis at hand, they will generate one. Even small situations escalate to create a sense of urgency and demand. You can hear them habitually saying, "If I don't do it, who will?"

A common symptom among co-dependent leaders is their failure to confront and deal with the inappropriate behaviours of others in the organization. They actually enable harmful or immoral behaviour. They fear hurting the feelings of others or having their approval ratings plummet. The key to failure is trying to please everybody. Does that mean a co-dependent leader needs to not care about what other people think? One expert says:

> No... I need not to care less what other people think but know more what I think and who I am, apart from what others think about me and who I think they think I am. In other words, the answer for those who tend to be driven by what others may or may not think of us, for those who tend to be hurt when others express disapproval or dislike, is to be self-differentiated. Differentiation is the ability to remain connected in relationship to significant people while choosing not to allow our behavior and our reactions to be determined by them... The differentiated person lives an "undivided life" by remaining true to his or her principles even though it may involve rejection or conflict.[30]

How do we know if we have an addiction of any sort, including co-dependency? Here are some simple questions to ask. Does this behaviour make me feel guilty or downcast? When I am downcast, do I often succumb to this behaviour? Does this activity require me to lie or make me feel embarrassed to admit I do it? If I neglect this behaviour, do I feel "off" or "on edge?" Does this activity interfere with my life, job, or relationships? Am I defensive about my participation in this behaviour?

Let's take this out of the leadership context for a moment and turn to relationships in general. My friend Tony is a retired police officer. He was telling me of a unique phenomenon that happens often, mostly on calls to domestic disputes. A spouse may call the police asking for assistance in controlling her abusive partner. On the scene, it is common for the spouse who made the emergency call to turn on the police and side with her mate. It is one of the most dangerous scenarios in policing.

This is co-dependency at work. In domestic situations, it is hard to convince a co-dependent that their belief that their abusive or addicted partner will change is unfounded. They believe the "It will never happen again" lie. In some cases they will actually take some of the blame for the abuser's or addict's behaviour. This is insecurity in its meanest form. The co-dependent begins to die inside, losing any sense of control or self-worth.

Sometimes I tease my friend's wife, saying, "When you get to heaven, there's a special medal just for you for marrying Joe." Their marriage is healthy, so it is fun to get Joe a little riled up. But in dysfunctional co-dependent relationships, saying similar things to the co-dependent actually encourages them. They feel championed, as a martyr for a noble cause. Others' pity brings them comfort.

Like with any addiction, no leader becomes a co-dependent instantly. Rather, it usually a progressive downward from a slight want to be needed to a full-blown messiah complex. Early in my leadership, I began down the path of co-dependency and fought my way back out. I learned as a young leader that I could gain approval by helping people with their struggles. Yes, this gave me leverage in leadership, but I found myself having emotional needs met in that manner. In a season of "putdowns" by some, I found myself gravitating to those who praised me for my assistance and leadership. I began to live in and for that world of validation.

It turned ugly, though, when I screwed up. Had my co-dependency progressed, I would have found myself tied to an emotionally demanding role. A vicious cycle would have begun where I tried harder to please but was continually left empty. Anger, hurt, disappointment, and resentment would have been the fallout.

For those infected with full-blown co-dependency, the build-up of emotional pain makes them compulsively focused on trying to control or transform their pain. A colleague of mine in this condition began to experience bizarre physical ailments and then had a mental breakdown. There were psychotic episodes, depression, and anxiety. His relationships were damaged. Thankfully, after walking through this "dark night of the soul", he rebounded successfully into a greater leadership capacity.

Moses was also a co-dependent leader. He was very dependent on those who were depending on him. It was so important for Jethro to intervene in Moses' life that he would otherwise have clearly burned out. I once heard someone wisely say that an inner compass must govern our leading, not a damp finger in the wind of public opinion.

The remedy for co-dependency is not easy. Defeating co-dependency is done by becoming more dependent on Christ. You must first establish healthy boundaries within your personal life, organization, and leadership. Next, learn to give away tasks. Delegate, empower, and give permission without intense meddling. Insecurity manifests itself in the ability to let others own their ministries or tasks. Lastly, listen to your spouse, children, and friends. If everyone is telling you that you are making a mistake, you are probably making a mistake!

I am not naïve about approval. I believe that to lead effectively you must be liked. A leader's likeability factor is a major component of leading well. However, when your security is based on what others think of you, you are sunk. We must not discount the admiration or dislike people feel towards us, but instead we should use that data for decision-making rather than for the determination of self-worth.

The Evil Opposite of Co-Dependency

Sean was fifteen years older than me and had been in leadership for over twenty years. If there is an opposite definition to co-dependency, he was it. Frankly, he did not care what people thought. On the outside he looked like a confident, visionary leader. People considered him a real man of action with many talents and a propensity to get things done.

It usually took six to twelve months in any leadership post before those he served wanted to drive him out. Because he lived in Canada, where niceness and grace abound, he got away with his behaviour for a long time.

He knew how to climb the ladder using people as the rungs. John Maxwell writes, "An important question for leaders: 'Am I building people, or building my dream and using people to do it?'"[31] Sean didn't mind conflict. I think he enjoyed it. It was neat to have such a leader at first, but people soon got weary of his narcissistic tendency. Jump to the end of the story: After a sexual moral failure, Sean now lives in isolation from family and friends.

If this reminds you of yourself, you must begin to be motivated a little more by the wishes of others. Bluntly, you need to care a little more about what other people think. It is difficult, maybe even impossible, to lead if you are not liked.

10

ROOTS

Why are so many people wasting their lives trying to change their pasts? You might as well give up all hope for a better past. If you only focus on what was, you will lose sight of what is and what could be. If you spend energy trying to fix your history, the only thing you will accomplish is the destruction of your future. If you are always comparing the past with the present, you will not see either clearly.

Everybody's childhood leaves a mark. There is a Chinese proverb that reads, "A child's life is like a piece of paper on which every passerby leaves a mark." Even if your childhood was void of trauma or abuse, the diverse challenges faced when growing up still leaves an effect. When we seek a better understanding of the significance of the key events in our lives, we are better able to discern the reasons for our insecurity. I like what one author said about these roots: "Roots always extend underground. Sometimes the only way we know one of these roots exists is when we see what's growing from it."[32]

There are various contributors to insecurity. Insecurities can be related to physical features, economic status, family background, academic achievements, and life experiences—the list doesn't stop there. These roots can be situational, emotional, contextual, psychological, chronic, cultural, national, or familial. I have categorized them into ten root causes, listed below.

Root Cause of Insecurity #1: Sin or Mistakes

William Wordsworth once wrote, "From the body of one guilty deed, a thousand ghostly fears and haunting thoughts proceed." There is no question that sins committed in the past echo into the future. Sometimes these raise the level of insecurity in our adult lives.

For all of us, our past mistakes vary in scope, strength, and size. Some linger. Some are easily forgotten. Determining which mistakes have "big" impacts is impossible because there are so many variables—like personality, character, and situation. Sometimes sin's influence into adulthood only has an effect if a repented adult has a faulty understanding of grace. There are often physical reminders, emotional scars, or painful memories. Sometimes we think we are "over it" only to see "it" surface again.

We tend to help people tackle the echo of past sins with cliché and Christianized rhetoric like, "When Satan reminds you of your past, remind him of his future." But it is not always that easy. We must be courageous enough to seek counsel and follow good advice. We must muster the courage to obey the Spirit's leading. Confess the sin, repent to God and any who have been wronged, and thereby release the stranglehold of sin. Do not choose sackcloth and ashes when He has given you the oil of joy. Enjoy grace! *"But God demonstrates his own love for us in this: While we were still sinners, Christ died for us."* (Romans 5:8). *"For it is by grace you have been saved, through faith—and this not from yourselves, it is the gift of God."* (Ephesians 2:8).

Root Cause of Insecurity #2: Drastic Change

There are all sorts of drastic change imposed on children and adolescents. These could be shifts in family wealth (standard of living), cultural shifts (rural to urban, or across international borders), or switching schools. All of these can provide soil for insecurity to germinate. On the other hand, drastic change can actually drive some people to be more confident and self-assured.

Children of military, police, and clergy are prone to move frequently. Foster children are often raised in multiple environments. Some of these grow into non-confident adults and others grow to be secure ones.

My father worked for the same company for thirty-five years and lived in the same town the entire time. Since retiring, he has begun to teach college students. I, however, since graduating from college sixteen years ago, have already worked in three different towns for three different employers. Statistics Canada tells us that workers will change jobs an average of ten times before they are forty years old.

Relocation is a common experience for many children. Approximately one in five American families move each year, which is higher than rates found in Great Britain, Germany, Japan, and other industrialized nations. In Canada, census figures indicate that almost half the population aged five and over have moved. Among movers, seventeen percent were children aged five to fourteen,[33] and the trend toward frequent relocation is on the rise.

There is evidence suggesting that young people who move frequently or have relocated recently are more likely than others to rank low on academic achievement, experiencing failure or dropping out altogether. They are more likely to be involved in theft, vandalism, sexual promiscuity, and drug abuse. Yet on the other side of the argument, several studies of the relocation adjustment problems among children have found that frequent moving sometimes leads to actual improvements in behaviour, enhancements in the quality of parent-child relations, and the development of more effective coping mechanisms.

Some researchers contend that adolescents are most vulnerable to the effects of moving because it often dissolves or weakens close friendships as well as relationships with others of the opposite sex. Since one's peer group is an important element in the development of adolescent self-worth, the cutting of ties with peers may lead to a sense of lost identity and insecurity. Life-event theorists consider "degree of personal control" over a particular event to be an important determinant of healthy psychological functioning in young people.

Root Cause of Insecurity #3: Religion

The generation that preceded mine villainized some cartoons like, for example, The Smurfs. After all, they were prone to using spells and dancing happily, not to mention their chauvinistic treatment of their single female, Smurfette. Our Sunday school teachers warned us about the consumption of evil breakfast cereals like Lucky Charms. And we spent our days fighting Popeye's peddling of candy cigarettes, debating the merits of Christian "rock," and whether or not Burt and Ernie had a same-gender attraction.

I have heard a similar testimony repeatedly from leaders, especially leaders whose teen years occurred in the 70s and 80s.

> My religious upbringing provided fertile soil for the growth of my dark side. The Pentecostal church I grew up in was one in which subtle legalism ruled the lives of its people. Because one's relationship with God was based to a great extent on behaviour, you were never quite sure where you stood spiritually after a week of being soiled by the sinful world. This lack of spiritual assurance led to repeated rededications each Sunday evening. It seemed that keeping God happy was a difficult and nearly impossible job—but it had to be done.[34]

Let's face it. We can be a tad selective and self-serving in our interpretations of Scripture. We embrace some rules and ignore others. What about tattoos and piercings? According to Leviticus 19:28, that hummingbird sketched onto your shoulder might have unpleasant eternal significance. How about poly-cotton? Is polyester a sin (Leviticus 19:19)? Yeah, you're right, it is—and not just because it is way too shiny. Bowl-cut hairdo? Nope, not allowed, according to Leviticus 19:27. It's a good thing the Second Coming didn't occur when I was seven. And, of course, the responsibilities of church ushers became very complicated with the institution of the "genitals required" rule of Deuteronomy 23:1. That's right: "No testicles. No service."

It is difficult not to be religious. It can be easy to walk around inside of religion and feel comfortable. Religion gives us a measuring stick by which we can see how we are doing and how others are doing, but it makes us into judges. Gregory Boyd said, "We are addicted to judgment."[35] Humiliating and passing judgment on others is a sneaky way of praising ourselves. But we like to judge. Our default mode is judgment, not grace. This allows us to get our sense of worth by adding or subtracting worth from others. Religion also gives us the tools to fool each other.

If you have been raised in a religious or legalistic environment, it is likely that you have insecure feelings of "not measuring up." Charles Swindoll writes:

> Being free, enjoying your liberty, and allowing others the same enjoyment is hard to do if you're insecure. It is especially hard to do

if you were raised by legalistic parents and led by legalistic pastors with an oversensitive conscience toward pleasing everyone. Those kinds of parents and pastors can be ultra-controlling, manipulative, and judgmental. Frequently they use the Bible as a hammer to pound folks into submission rather than as a guide to lead others into grace. Sometimes it takes years for people who have been under a legalistic cloud to finally have the courage to walk freely in the grace of God.[36]

Root Cause of Insecurity #4: Parents or Parenting

One of the major factors that lead to insecurity lies in childhood distress. Lack of love from one or both parents, being brought up by a single parent, or growing up viewing a bad relationship between parents affects a person's psyche, resulting in future difficulty trusting the people you're in relationships with.

The parenting years is such a long season, combined with the fact that no one will ever influence your life like your parents, means those years played a primary role in your level of adult security. Because of the resiliency of human nature, it is unlikely that a single event created insecurity. But the accumulation of experiences in your home plus the parenting you received accounts for much of who you are today. For example, if your parents taught you that "good enough" was never good enough, you might carry that into adulthood as insecurity.

Let me give you a few other examples of parenting behaviours or omissions that may come together to generate insecurity. One of the biggest is stability. If your parents failed to provide you with emotional or physical stability, you may have grown up to be "on edge." Sure, children are adaptable to change, but not as much as we have been tricked into thinking. They do not easily recover from neglect, abuse, or broken attachments. What children *are* good at, in many cases, is burying their feelings only to see them emerge at a later date. (It must be noted that some parents try to appease their own consciences by excessively giving their children material items. In many cases, this only aggravates the problem.)

Stability is created by predictability. Families that have a suppertime routine or a bedtime ritual tend to raise more secure kids. Churchgoing kids obviously have the advantage of being in a faith community and learning to put their trust in the Lord, but they also benefit from the tradition of weekly Sunday services. Rituals like teeth brushing or hugging your kids before you leave for work speaks volumes to children about their security.

Traditions give children a sense of identity. When children get to participate in family traditions, they subconsciously hear the message that everything is okay. In our home, we made a decision to always be in our own home for Christmas morning. Parents and relatives are always welcome to join us, but we wanted our kids to have a memory of always being together as a family on key occasions. As well, for Christmas, Easter, and other special events, there are specific procedures and protocols known only to us.

I do not have any scientific research to prove this, but I believe the biggest key to effective parenting has nothing to do with parenting at all. I think it has much to do with being a loving spouse. There is no greater source of stability and security for a child than to know that Dad loves Mom. In our busy household, when I walk through the door, coming home from work or a trip, it's my kids who usually greet me. But one of my first questions to them is, "Where's mom?" They know I love her and they probably think I love her more than them. I do not want my kids to ever wonder if Mom and Dad are going to stick together.

Root Cause of Insecurity #5: Life Experiences

A few summers ago, I was driving our small car through a lonely little village near our home. Rounding a bend, I watched a transport truck with a steel container attached come toward me. It was tipping over onto its driver side wheels. Then, slowly, it tipped fully onto its side landed just in front of my car. Feeling like a superhero, I jumped from the car and kicked in the truck's front window. (The windows are *meant* to pop out easily, but I still felt like a superhero.) I got in the cab to find the driver shaken but not injured. He was pinned there, so we sat and chatted for fifteen minutes before emergency vehicles arrived. He kept repeating, "I don't understand. I was going slow!" And indeed he was driving slowly around the turn. I asked him what he was hauling. He did not know.

After they freed the driver, we were able to examine the contents of the container. It was a load of poorly stacked heavy steel tubes. Although the speed into the turn was low, it was just enough for the load to shift. The shift of the internal load produced a catastrophic external result. The driver may have driven hundreds of kilometres without incident, but when a number of factors (speed, angle of turn, pitch of the road) aligned just right, his truck tipped.

Many people cruise through life with unsecured cargo. Some people crash quickly. Some never crash. Some, when the factors are just right (or wrong), are surprised to find their lives toppling over; they are surprised at the tragedy because they thought they were "doing just fine" or had travelled so long without incident. The baggage in your hold must be dealt with. It may not be removable, but it can be fastened down. The baggage we carry in life only grows heavier as we get older. It puts us out of balance, perhaps a little at first, then sharply at times of stress or crisis.

Cargo of Rejection. Rejection is a powerful root of insecurity. A friend of mine who is a fantastic leader and author wrote an exceptional book a few years ago entitled *Thundering Silence.* He tells his life story of parental rejection and how he navigated through the emotional implications that followed him into adulthood. Ross writes about his father:

> When [my father] was ninety-six I travelled over to visit with the hope of engaging him in some meaningful conversation. My wife and I arrived at the seniors' home around eleven thirty in the morning. We were given his room number at the nurses' station. We came to his room and walked inside. He was sitting on the end of his bed, reading a newspaper. I walked over to him and said, "Hello, Father, how are you?" He looked up, a puzzled look on his face, and then recognized me saying, "is that you Ross?" I assured him that it was indeed me and that we had arrived early the day before. He then looked at his watch and said, "Gosh, what a time to come—it's lunchtime." Without another word he reached for his walker, walked past us, left the room, and proceeded to the cafeteria.[37]

There are as many forms of rejection as there are ways in which people respond to it. Social rejection (as a child or adolescent). Professional rejection (being overlooked for promotions or new jobs). Academic rejection (poor school grades or denial of entrance into college). Familial rejection (from siblings or relatives). Parental rejection (parents left or ignored you). Canine rejection (Ruffles, the family pet, had nothing to do with you). Whatever the case, you have your own list of rejections. How are they impacting you today? I have met adults who are still trying to prove themselves to someone from their past. Sometimes the person from whom they want acceptance is not even living anymore!

We will talk more about this later, but for now you must believe Isaiah 41:9: "—*I took you from the ends of the earth, from its farthest corners I called you. I said, 'You are my servant'; I have chosen you and have not rejected you.*"

Cargo of Wounds. Wounds hurt, obviously. More than that, they make an impression on our psyche. That's how we learned that a sharp object can cut skin or that a kettle can be hot. (Even when I know that the stove element is not hot, I still hover my hand over it before I touch it—just to make sure.) My three boys were all stubborn as toddlers, probably a trait they picked up from their mother. "Don't touch it. It's hot!" was usually interpreted as, "Touch it. See if Dad is telling the truth." These impressions are good things. They sometimes keep us from new injury and pain.

Sandy and I went white-water rafting in Maine a few years back. The trip was exciting and enjoyable until we neared the end. We had to descend though a Class IV series of rapids. I was not sure what Class IV meant, but now I know it's the class of rapids somewhere between stupid and suicidal. Pause. I just "Googled" it. According to Wikipedia, it means, "Whitewater, large waves, long rapids, rocks, maybe a considerable drop, sharp manoeuvres may be needed. (Skill Level: Whitewater Experience)."

We descended the rapid without capsizing. While we were waiting for others, we directed our boat into a "water hydraulic" where you, theoretically, position your raft in such a way that the back-flow keeps your boat stationary even while in swift water. Our guide said it was possible. He lied. The raft flipped and Sandy and I found ourselves in the cold drink. Worse than that, when our lifejackets took us to the surface, we came up under the raft. As I pulled myself to the side, the boat shifted and put me back under the center of the boat. My thought was, "*Hmm. I never thought this would be the way I would die.*" Sandy popped up near the raft somehow. I bobbed to the surface twenty or thirty feet downriver, glad to be alive and to see Sandy being safely pulled into the boat. Once aboard, Sandy cried. I could have cried, but I didn't because I am a tough and fearless outdoorsman. I am. Just ask anyone who doesn't know me.

When the opportunity to go white-water rafting came again the next year, Sandy declined graciously. I, however, signed up for a second run. What surprised me is how much tighter I held on, and how I switched from the normal sitting on the edge position (supposedly the correct one) to moving more to the center of the boat. I now knew the risks at hand and I craved the security of the center of the craft. Like they say, much of good judgment comes from bad experience, and a lot of that comes from bad judgment.

Wounds are powerful producers of insecurity. Caxton has translated the moral of one of Aesop's stories, "He that hath ben ones begyled by somme other ought to kepe hym wel from the same." From that fable was birthed the phrase, "Once bitten, twice shy." Take a look at your bite wounds. Are you shying away from things as a result? Yes, we are products of our experiences, but we don't have to be prisoners of them. Your scars might remind you of your painful experiences, but it is important that they also remind you that your wound was not fatal.

I have noticed a few common occurrences in the lives of leaders who have unresolved wounds. They are:

1. Prone to anger—Outbursts of rage occur, tempers flare, and personal attacks ensue.
2. Habitually sinning—The leader continues to struggle, repeatedly, with substance addictions, pornography, inappropriate relationships, gossip, and sinful attitudes.
3. Frequently Sick—The psychological and spiritual weight of unhealed wounds produces consistent and frequent illness and negative biological effects.
4. Quarrelsome—They enjoy conflict and are often in conflict over the same issues.
5. Negative—Complaints, blame, and criticism dominates behaviour.
6. Isolated—Connection to others is diminished or absent.

Cargo of Loss. The loss of a person in one's life can provide a lifetime of insecurity for people who live in fear that loss will visit them again. They can become paranoid, overcautious, and protective. With almost half of today's young people experiencing the loss of a parent through divorce, [38] we have yet to see how this epidemic will impact future leaders. These young people are at increased risk for depression, anxiety, and behavioural problems, receiving bad grades or leaving school earlier, becoming young offenders, or experiencing their own relationship problems down the road.

Loss that comes in the form of death, especially the death of a parent or a close family member, is usually the most significant. While I was attending a leadership school, we were asked to share what really drives us to strive to lead and why we want to lead well. Some of the answers were predictable—wanting to help the needy, change the world, leave a legacy, make the community a better place, and so forth. I have forgotten all of my other thirty classmates' responses, except Steve's. Stifling his emotion as much as possible, Steve confessed that his desire to make a difference was fuelled by the loss of his brother in a plane crash. "I've wanted to prove to God that I was worth keeping alive and that I would redeem my brother's death by leading and working enough for both of us," he said. A beautiful moment followed as a young leader let go of something that could have swallowed him slowly in the muck of misappropriated drivenness.

There are many forms of loss, and not all loss is necessarily the absence of a beloved person. Significant loss could also be a monetary loss or the loss of a home or object. All loss has an impact. Stop reading for a minute and take an inventory of your life's losses. How are those losses colouring your life and leadership today?

"Artificial security" can result from an attachment of any kind, even one that seems relatively minor. Do you have anything in your life that provides a false sense of security?

Root Cause of Insecurity #6: Family Relationships

Siblings. Your brothers and sisters—more specifically, how they treat you—have a direct impact on your sense of security. The way your parents treated them, as opposed to you, has an even more marked influence. Imagine what James' life was like as the brother of the Saviour of the world. In a way, James could have seen a gross inequity between himself and Jesus. But instead of being jealous of Jesus, James arguably became Jesus' closest ally. When Jesus arrived at the house of Jairus, he did not let anyone go in with him except Peter, John, James, and the child's father and mother. "Later Jesus took Peter, *James* and John along with him, and he began to be deeply distressed and troubled." (Mark 14:33)

Birth Order. Much has been written about the influence of birth order and it affects a person's psychological make-up and the level of insecurity they might possess. To understand more fully the impact of birth order on self-esteem, self-worth, and confidence, there are many resources available.[39]

In *The Leader's Journey*, the authors conclude:

> Each child grows up in a different family, depending on his or her configuration in that family. The oldest child may have parents who are vigilant and idealistic, while the youngest child in the same family usually has a mother and father who are more relaxed, indulgent, less restrictive, and more tired. Older children may have more of the parents' time and attention, while the family may have more resources available for the younger children.
>
> As we grow up interacting with our brothers and sisters, we learn who we are in relation to other people. We learn to dominate and submit, to placate and compromise, to lead and follow. We learn how to relate to members of the same sex and the opposite sex. We can even predict how a person learns to react to anxiety by looking at the place in the family that he or she occupies.[40]

Marriage. Your spouse is the single greatest influence on your level of insecurity or confidence. The comments and actions of our spouses mean the most to us. When we are put down, we feel low. When we are admired, loved, and respected, our confidence rises. Insecurity rises when a spouse neglects spending time with their partner, fails to touch him or her, avoids serving him or her in life tasks, or generally seems unhappy. With our wild imaginations, we concoct crazy thoughts about what our spouse thinks or doesn't think about us. Jealousy can increase. Fear can grow.

Some worry that they are not worthy of their partner's love or attention. They feel inferior. Of course, this leads to a strong sense that one's spouse may leave for someone else. Spouses may have fear that someone else is more present in their partner's life. Marriage insecurity can only be defeated by the constant expression of unconditional love and extensive verbal and non-verbal communication.

Sex. Sex has a direct impact on a man's security and confidence. Some women do not understand the importance of sex for their husbands. To understand it as purely physical is to misunderstand the deep emotional impact for men. Women see how cranky men get when sex is not frequent, and women know sex can be used as a weapon or a bargaining tool, but I have met a number of women who do not connect the dots between sex and security. Some women cannot see the connection between such a physical act and the male emotional need. Sex is not all about physical pleasure for men. A husband can go quite a while without the pleasure of sex. What they can't survive is the neglect of the emotional need that sex satisfies. I know it sounds kind of "sissy" in a culture where men are not portrayed as emotional creatures, but it is true.

Now, I know that men do not understand a lot of the complexities of females, so I will avoid any attempt to explain that aspect of the equation. Unlike men, women are mystifying creatures. Men have two basic needs: sex and sandwiches. Pretty simple. But those things, as weird or "wrong" as they might seem, have a lot of influence. Sex says, "I love you," "I'm attracted to you," and "Our relationship is safe." You may say those things, but your man doesn't put much stock in those words if you are making a conscious decision to avoid sex.

It may be that denying a man sex is fitting revenge for his inattentiveness to his wife's needs, but the message communicated probably has more significance than the woman may think. What he hears is, "I reject you. You are not good enough." Simply, it makes him feel less of a man and lowers his self-worth.

I spoke with several women about what men do that may cause a woman to feel insecure. Below is a sampling of some of their responses.

"While in mixed company, a husband is always heard talking about how wonderful a friend's wife is and all the things she does. Correcting how his wife does things, even simple things like folding laundry or cooking or keeping house."

"Not making date nights or creating special moments."

"Not spontaneously telling her he loves her."

"Discounting the work she does outside the home and in, by coming across as if his schedule and events are more important."

"Hanging with 'the guys' on a more regular basis than with his wife."

"Keeping close relationships with women he knew before getting married."

"One thing my husband is good at is making me feel secure in our relationship. If there was anything that made me feel insecure it would be that he does not follow up his words with actions. This is probably the case for a lot of men, but William is good at saying, "I love you," but not good at showing it. So how do I know he really loves me if his actions don't say it? I need more than words to let me know things are good. He could be saying the right words, and then going behind my back and showing someone else the right actions (which I know he isn't doing), but words are so easy for men to say, but actions is where the real truth lies."

"When I don't have verbal feedback and he gets quiet - I feel insecure...it leaves me wondering, 'what is he thinking?' and then I try to think of what he might be thinking."

"When I feel that he is short with me in front of his friends. (This is rare and hasn't happened in a while but when it happens it miffs me off)."

"When we MAJORLY disagree on something VERY important to me."

"When I hear ZERO feedback - positive or negative about something I've done."

Root Cause of Insecurity #7: Physical Attributes

Disability. Personal limitations such as a learning disability, physical handicap, or anything that makes us feel different or inferior can play into insecurity.

Stature. It is rumoured that people who are short, especially males, tend to overcompensate in others areas of life. In an article entitled "Napoleon Complex," Wikipedia reports, "Professor Abraham Buunk of the University of Groningen in the Netherlands has found evidence of the small man syndrome. Researchers at the University found that men who were 5'4" were 50% more likely to show signs of jealousy than men who were 6'6". Sociological experiments have shown that there are several advantages to being tall, including attracting a mate, and the small man syndrome is believed by some to be an evolutionary adaptation."[41]

Appearance. Some faces are made for movies and some are made for radio. "Good looks" have been proven to accelerate one's career and open up more options in relationships.

Root Cause of Insecurity #8: Temperament

Three professionals were arrested and convicted of a crime. Among them was a doctor, a lawyer, and an engineer. They were led to the guillotine one by one. The crowd was roaring with anticipation. First up was the doctor. The doctor was placed in the guillotine and the lanyard was yanked. The blade started on its massive, merciless drop down and lurched to a stop just inches above the doctor's neck. The official in charge declared that it would be inhumane to make the doctor suffer this way more than once, so he set the doctor free. The crowd howled. The executioner checked his equipment. All seemed to be in order. Then the lawyer was placed in the guillotine and the blade was released. Again, the blade stopped partway down! The presiding official once again said that he would set this prisoner free because of the unusual circumstances. The crowd screamed in frustration. Now came the engineer. The crowd fell silent. The executioner rechecked his equipment. As the engineer was marched up to the guillotine, he looked carefully at it, and said, "Wait, I see the problem!"

Some people are determined to receive the short end of the stick! Simply put, some personalities are more prone to insecurity than others. Dr. Nowinski calls this "the tender heart," or sensitive person. He writes:

> We each possess a unique personality, which is the outcome of the dispositions we are born with plus the experiences we have had. What many people would like to know, and what they need to know in order to understand and help themselves, is precisely what combination of disposition and experience can explain such profoundly different personalities, and therefore such vastly different responses. Only by knowing the answer to that question can people take action to prevent themselves or others from the debilitating reaction that the [insecure person] had.[42]

He goes on to say that another factor in determining whether we will become insecure is the type of disposition we are born with:

> Depending on how severe they are and when they happen, some losses have the potential to affect almost all of us in very negative ways. Certain traumatic experiences, in other words, have the potential to make most of us at least a little insecure. More typically, though, experience in and of itself does not entirely account for insecurity. If it did, then everyone who's been exposed to some loss or abuse would be equally insecure, and we know this is not the case.[43]

Root Cause of Insecurity #9: Media or Culture

We do not need surveys or a study to tell us that modern media is affecting the confidence levels of children, teenagers, and adults. Common sense tells us that pop culture is causing a big problem. Films, magazines, photographs, and television shows make people feel unattractive and less desirable. Media teaches young female teenagers that to be sensual and sexual is to be secure and powerful.

One website reports:

> Stereotypes formed by the media that include thin, tanned women, and wealthy, muscular men have led to a decline in self-acceptance. The majority of advertisers today often present the perfect body to the public, hoping that consumers will strive to achieve attractiveness using a certain product or idea. While this form of advertising may somewhat increase a product's market share, many people suffer from inner conflicts as a result of failure to achieve the body of an athlete or fashion model. Along with emotional conflicts, those influenced by the media have encountered physical problems, including bulimia, anorexia, and the employment of harmful dietary plans. Unless reality is discerned from what is presented in certain media, some people will continue to suffer. Consumers could find the truth more easily if media offered products advertised by normal people without all the extra glamour. In addition to this, if the public could view advertising only as something to get one's attention and not a portrayal of how one should look, there

would be fewer problems. Until either is accomplished, the negative effects will be felt by the vulnerable, and companies will continue to make their money.[44]

Modern media is a major source of fuel for the insecurity epidemic.

People are not just growing up insecure; they are downright scared! Movie and television themes often feature excessive violence. By the time a child turns eighteen, he or she will have witnessed 16,000 murders and 200,000 acts of violence on television alone.

Consider this: if a person spends two hours per day watching television, that equals one twelfth of his or her 24-hour day. That means one month of each year is spent in front of the television. The average television viewer is spending approximately 28 to 32 hours per week watching television. Thus, Canadians spend over two months a year watching television. Now mix in the use of the internet, video games, and movies. This makes the media a highly influential force in a person's life.

Brandon Centerwall surveyed a group of men in prison for violent crime and found nearly one-third of the inmates had consciously imitated a crime technique they had seen in the media.[45] People possibly learn more about life through television than any other source.

Root Cause of Insecurity #10: Psychological

I visited the home of a young, bright pastor who was experiencing much success in his local church ministry. Despite his achievement, he was newly afflicted with panic disorder. The attacks were bad enough to keep him from going to grocery stores or restaurants. His fear level (insecurity) rose to a crippling level.

A high-stress and high-demand environment ignited his disorder. Some disorders are genetic and some people are genetically prone to them. There are a plethora of psychiatric disorders, and those who possess them often feel insecure or inferior. Our society has a lot of progress to make in reducing the stigma associated with mental illness. Society still behaves that mental illness is something you "just shake off" or "suck up"—that's *discouragement*. Clinical *depression* is biological, and usually genetic. It is a disease just like diabetes or gallstones, and therefore deserves no stigma. Usually, those with depression, obsessive-compulsive disorder, anorexia, bulimia, social anxiety, or phobias feel shame. For this reason, most people avoid treatment.

An insecure person might not necessarily have insecurity as their root issue. Anyone trying to tackle insecurity must first deal with any presenting mental illness. Insecurity is often misunderstood when the real problem is clinical depression. Depression is the "common cold" of mental illness, with twenty-five percent of people experiencing it during their lifetime. However, it is very treatable.

Treatment for depression usually involves increasing levels of serotonin in the brain. Medications are available that attempt to specifically target and increase serotonin. These are known as Selective Serotonin Reuptake Inhibitors (SSRI's).

Perhaps the best way to think of serotonin is again with an automobile example. Most automobiles in Canada are made to cruise at a hundred kilometres per hour, which is perfect for highways. If we place that same automobile on a racetrack and drive day after day at two hundred kilometres per hour, two things would happen—parts would fail and we would run the engine so hot as to evaporate or burnout the oil. Serotonin is the brain's "oil."

Like a normal automobile on a racetrack, when we find ourselves living in a high-stress situation for a prolonged period of time, we use more serotonin than can normally be replaced. Imagine a list of your pressures, responsibilities, difficulties, and environmental issues (difficult job, bad marriage, poor housing, rough neighbourhood, etc.). Prolonged exposure to such a high level of stress gradually lowers our serotonin level. As we continue to "hang on," we develop symptoms of severe stress-induced depression.

An automobile can be one, two, or three litres low on oil. Imagine that brain serotonin can have similar stages, being low (one litre low), moderately low (two litres low), and severely low (three litres low). The less serotonin is available in the brain, the more severe our depression and related symptoms.[46]

The main symptom of depression is a sad, despairing mood that is present most days, lasts most of the day, and persists for more than two weeks. It impairs one's performance at work, at school, or in social relationships.

Other symptoms may include changes in appetite and weight, sleep problems, and loss of interest in work, hobbies, people, or sex. Withdrawal from family members and friends and feeling useless, hopeless, excessively guilty, pessimistic, or irritable can also be signs. Most depressed people feel fatigue and have trouble concentrating, remembering, and making decisions. They cry easily or feel like crying but are unable to. In more severe cases, depressed people may have thoughts of suicide and possess a loss of touch with reality, hearing voices (hallucinations) or having strange ideas (delusions).

Leaders should consult their doctor if they experience any of these symptoms or if they think you may have a mental illness.

• • •

> We cannot change the circumstances of our childhood, much less improve them at this later date, but we can recall them honestly, reflect on them, understand them, and thereby overcome their influence on us. Withdrawal can return to hope, compulsion to will, in addition to purpose, and inertia to confidence through the exercise of memory and understanding.[47]

The roots listed above are reasons. They are not excuses. They are listed above for understanding, not justification. Don't believe the lie that your history will also be your destiny. As Lutzer said, "Every saint has a past; every sinner has a future."[48]

After a long flight from the East Coast of Canada to the West Coast, I arrived late at night to my hotel in Vancouver. At check-in, the clerk told me that I did not have a reservation—by now it was 2:00 a.m. (6:00 a.m. body clock time). I knew a reservation had been made, but they had no record of it. After fifteen minutes of checking the computer, arguing, checking spelling, and swapping confirmation numbers, I finally gave in. The clerk was pleased to win the argument. I accepted that I had no reservation and began eyeing the sofa in the hotel lobby. Then the clerk informed me that there were rooms available, even without a reservation. I groaned inside. We had become so focused on who was at fault that we became more interested in the problem than the solution. Don't let this happen to you on your journey toward security.

11

REMEDY

It was twenty-five years and 120 pounds ago, but I still remember the first time I was called "fat." I know where I was standing. I can even recall the colour of the walls. I also remember where I was when my new glasses earned me the nickname "four-eyes." Historical events like these that have no impact are still stored on the hard drive of my mind. All of us, with only a few neurological mouse clicks, can locate these scenes and words etched in our minds. Our brains can retrieve those insults quickly and, often without intention, they can embed themselves into our spirit. While there may be some element of truth in some of these "scripts" (things said to us about us), leaders suffer when tethered to the negative ones.

Jordan was a young leader I met shortly before he quit leadership. He had been told all his life that he was destined for greatness, and he was, but not in the spotlight sort of way he wanted. He had talent and personality that seemed to point to greatness. The problem was, he was average. His talent was too narrow to match what he perceived leadership to be. His personality was a little "over the top."

Along the way, he began to understand greatness as "fame." Respect and prominence became the indicators of whether or not he was successful, even though he knew better. He was a very good leader, but whenever he didn't receive the reverence he expected from his followers it would trigger his insecurity and he would spend days feeling frustrated and victimized.

In a day when the mantra is "It's my parents' fault," we might be quick to blame Jordan's family and friends, but the truth is that it's Jordan's fault. There may have been some faulty scripts in his journey, but his refusal to process through his tendencies was ultimately what did him in. If we refuse to explore and acknowledge our proneness to specific issues, we condemn ourselves to the mercy of pride and arrogance.

On trips to Thailand, I have always been amazed at how the elephant is revered and treasured. In Thailand I am astounded by the amount of elephant-shaped paraphernalia I see everywhere I go. There are endless carvings, statues, and other keepsakes in the form of elephants. Elephants have a deep religious meaning there. Legend has it that Buddha's mother had a dream about a white elephant before he was born, and the Hindu god Ganesha is said to have the head of an elephant, symbolizing intelligence, because the elephant is so smart.

Historically, elephants in Thailand were used for clearing forests, making it easy for people to open up trade routes. Today, elephants are seldom used for logging, but they are popular with tourists. One can even watch an elephant painting a picture of another elephant!

They say, "An elephant never forgets." They are known for their fantastic memories and are especially smart. But despite their intellect and enormity, an elephant that has been in captivity since birth is usually easy to restrain. Trainers use only a small stake in the ground and a piece of rope. Even full-grown elephants are held with the same small restraint! When captive elephants are young, their trainers stake them down. After hundreds of attempts to pull away from the stake, the baby elephant learns that it cannot get loose. That truth is 'burned' into their memory. As adults, they still believe more in the strength of the stake than they do in their own capacity for magnificent power.

People, too, are often "staked." Some person, study, or program has told them they are too poor or too small or too old or have some other condition that makes some achievements out of reach. Some leaders are staked down by the words spoken to them in the early days of leadership development or during childhood.

Sometimes leaders etch their own damaging scripts, but usually it is some insensitive or mistaken "trainer" who drives a psychological or spiritual stake that confines them for years. "You're a follower, not a leader." "You are too shy to speak in front of crowds." "You are not really good under pressure." "You're too awkward." "Too clumsy." "Too poor." "Not smart enough." "You have no business sense." "Forgetful." "Can't be trusted." "You didn't try hard enough." "Don't let them see that you are weak." Scripts like these burn into the psyche and taint leadership ability. Those lies echo for years.

Dr. Chris Thurman writes,

> Far too many of us get both our identity and our worth from the various roles we play. Our identity may come from "I'm a parent" or "I'm a teacher." Our worth then comes from how well we perform in those roles. Letting our identity come from the roles we play and allowing our worth to come from how well we play those roles are two humongous mistakes… Your identity is not "loser," "idiot," "failure," or "wimp." Your identity is "child of God," "saint," "heir," and "new creation." When you assume the wrong identity, you lose not only an accurate sense of who you are but all the emotional and spiritual health that goes with it. When you have the correct identity, you don't have to find one in a role you play (spouse, parent, worker, friend) or buy into false identities that may have been handed to you by somebody else.[49]

Let me add a brief side note. There exists an obvious challenge—to watch what we say. That includes the scripts we speak in the form of teasing or sarcasm. In fact, it is a bad habit to rebuke or correct a person's behaviour by joking, teasing, or being sarcastic. We should seek the courage to communicate important messages with straight talk and caring conversation. *"Words kill, words give life; they're either poison or fruit—you choose"* (Proverbs 18:21, The Message).

I recently read a blog from an anonymous teen writer and the headline caught my attention: "You spend your whole life… trying to live up to what your parents expect you to be." Although the understanding of parental expectation and encouragement of the teen is flawed, she goes on to write some interesting thoughts:

> Life is so hard for me but no one sees it. I'm trying harder than you all think I am, but no one sees it. I have a game plan and it is actually a really good one, but no one sees it. I feel like things used to come so easy in life but now the game changed. God switched up the rules and I'm starting to lose. Why can't I just go back? Start all over and re-do things. Unfortunately life does not come with a reset button. I admit I am afraid. Afraid to grow up. Afraid to leave home. Afraid to die. Afraid I'm going to fail. When you are constantly being told you are going nowhere in life… it really starts to eat at you. Slowly chewing you up inside, making you numb. You start to feel nothing. You turn to drugs thinking, "What do I have to lose? My life? I'm already dead anyway." When life gets like this who do you turn to? God? I feel bad but I'm starting to doubt His power. It seems like my whole life He has not been here.[50]

The danger of embracing a harmful script is that it amplifies fear. We live in a world that trades on fear. I just saw a television commercial that actually said, "[Product] reduces the risk of death by 21%."

When we give a negative script the attention it seeks, we get scared, stop taking risks, and cease trying to take new ground. We continue in the leadership role with no heart for it. We become depleted emotionally, spiritually, relationally, and physically. Feelings become mistaken for facts.

There are some common clues: The leader often is bothered when someone else is recognized for achievement or has a stroke of good fortune. They tend to be hyper-aware of themselves or unusually self-conscious. When they are criticized it causes an emotional tailspin or a lengthy rumination that lasts abnormally long. And there is a recurring sense that the person lives with a constant, overarching belief that they don't measure up. Thus the fear of criticism stifles his or her creativity and innovation.

There are principles for handling negative scripts. *First, acknowledge the truth (if any) in the script, process it, and then toss the rest away.* These scripts will then remain in memory but do not have to continue to resonate in one's leadership. If we are going to lead well, these forces cannot be permitted to continue shaping our identity. We would become unsafe people to follow.

Next, redirect the script. Like the principles taught in martial arts, redirect the force and use it against your opponent (in this case the satanic forces, not the individual). Paul writes to the Corinthians:

[God's] strength comes into its own in your weakness. Once I heard that, I was glad to let it happen. I quit focusing on the handicap and began appreciating the gift. It was a case of Christ's strength moving in on my weakness. Now I take limitations in stride, and with good cheer, these limitations that cut me down to size—abuse, accidents, opposition, bad breaks. I just let Christ take over! And so the weaker I get, the stronger I become. (2 Corinthians 12:9–10, The Message)

Our faults are often what make us attractive and empower us as leaders. Nobody wants to follow a leader who has it all together (or thinks he or she has it all together). Authenticity trumps all other leadership skill as long as the leader does not use authenticity as an excuse to cease to grow.

Write new scripts. Let me discuss and clarify some new scripts throughout the remaining chapters as remedial steps toward security. If we can say these scripts with honesty, we are well on our way to confident leadership.

Lastly, be positive and optimistic. A little boy wearing his baseball cap and toting a ball and bat was overheard talking to himself as he strutted through the backyard: "I'm the greatest hitter in the world!" Then he tossed the ball into the air, swung at it, and missed.

"Strike one!" he yelled.

Undaunted, he picked up the ball and said again, "I'm the greatest hitter in the world!" He tossed the ball into the air. When it came down he missed again.

"Strike two!" he cried.

The boy then paused a moment to examine his bat and ball carefully. He spit on his hands and rubbed them together. He straightened his cap and said once more, "I'm the greatest hitter in the world!"

Again he tossed the ball up in the air and swung at it. He missed. "Strike Three!"

"Wow! Strike three," he exclaimed. Then, "Wow! I'm the greatest pitcher in the world!"

Attitude is everything. Optimists and pessimists are both likely to be correct.

In the following chapters, we will look at the scripts that serve to remedy insecurity.

12

ABIDING

"Inquietum est cor nostrum donec requiescat in Te"
(Restless is our heart until it rests in Thee)

Augustine

Life Script #1: "Apart from Jesus, I can do nothing."

Take a moment to read John 15. Wait. Read it! Don't just skip over the Bible verse like we normally do when scriptures appear in a book. This passage is rich in leadership lessons. Pick the lessons out as you read:

> I am the true vine, and my Father is the gardener. He cuts off every branch in me that bears no fruit, while every branch that does bear fruit he prunes so that it will be even more fruitful. You are already clean because of the word I have spoken to you. Remain in me, and I will remain in you. No branch can bear fruit by itself; it must remain in the vine. Neither can you bear fruit unless you remain in me.
>
> I am the vine; you are the branches. If a man remains in me and I in him, he will bear much fruit; apart from me you can do nothing. If anyone does not remain in me, he is like a branch that

is thrown away and withers; such branches are picked up, thrown into the fire and burned. If you remain in me and my words remain in you, ask whatever you wish, and it will be given you. This is to my Father's glory, that you bear much fruit, showing yourselves to be my disciples.

As the Father has loved me, so have I loved you. Now remain in my love. If you obey my commands, you will remain in my love, just as I have obeyed my Father's commands and remain in his love. I have told you this so that my joy may be in you and that your joy may be complete. My command is this: Love each other as I have loved you. (John 15:1–12)

The term "abiding" is now archaic but its' meaning is a key to confident leadership. If it is not *His* ministry, we cannot give true leadership. Without Him we can build great empires and enterprises, but they will not last. It leaves me wondering why we ask God to help us with *our* ministry. Shouldn't it be the other way around? Isn't it His ministry, and aren't we helping Him?

Sometimes we are guilty of letting our pride drive us past the call of God. Let me ask it this way: How at peace are you? Is your soul resting and abiding in the Vine? Augustine said, "You have made us for Yourself, and our hearts are restless until they find their rest in You."[51] I have had my share of struggle with "abiding." Drivenness and busyness have plagued me, but I have learned (and am still learning) that all this isn't for me. It is for Christ and His cause.

I had a meaningful moment happen during a conference I was leading. A young leader approached me and offered an apology for his recent behaviour—behaviour that I was not aware of. He said, "Jim, I apologize for believing what everyone is saying about you." I'm not sure that qualifies as an apology, because it sounded to me like a covert way of baiting me into an argument. Nonetheless, I knew I had made some progress in the area of abiding when I instinctively shook his hand, looked him in the eye, and thanked him for his apology. My former self would have quickly asked, "What are they saying about me?" But it didn't matter now. I knew I was living out what Christ had called me to do, and doing it to the best of my ability.

It is a waste of time to argue with your opponents. I had to learn to leave my reputation to God and try to focus on my own calling. Steve Brown wrote in *No More Mr. Nice Guy*, "Did you know that studies have shown that it is almost impossible to give a dog an ulcer? Do you know why? Because dogs hardly ever try to be anything but a dog."[52]

Sandy and I once owned a big blue Ford truck. It was a monster. It worked great, except the gas gauge was broken and I was too cheap to fix it. More than once I got a phone call from an angry wife calling from a stranger's phone to let me know she was stranded on the side of the road. We need gauges in our life, and we need to pay attention to them.

I once attended a seminar led by Carson Pue, President of Arrow Leadership International and author of *Mentoring Leaders*. He touched on the subject of abiding and cited some common occurrences for those who do not learn this. They are worth listing here as gauges for our level of "abiding":

Burn-out is a clinical condition caused by over-commitment, pressure, an internal desire to please, and an external desire to succeed. Its victim is often fooled by ongoing fruitfulness. The result is emotional, physical, relational, and spiritual depletion.

Drop-out results in unfulfilled dreams, discouragement and disillusionment. Often the leader is guilty of continuing in the ministry role with no heart for it or they find personal fulfillment in another area.

Levelling-out occurs when a person reaches a plateau and stops growing as a leader. This is often due to an inability to resolve certain life issues or a loss of faith that God will actually do anything.

Fall-out is usually caused by unmet emotional needs. The leader participates in escapist sin due to a desire to satisfy hollowness within. The leader falls to sins of money, sex, power, and/or substance abuse. Often, he or she has a well-polished public image but have two identities.

Spread-out occurs when a leader dabbles in a wide array of activities. This is especially difficult for multi-gifted leaders. He or she lacks focus, which leaves an increasing sense of dissatisfaction. David Kraft, in *Leaders Who Last*, writes:

> In the relentless busyness of modern life, we have lost the rhythm between action and rest. There is a universal refrain: I am so busy. As it all piles endlessly upon itself, the whole experience of being alive begins to melt into one enormous obligation. Realize the difference between a concern and a responsibility. Sabbath time is a revolutionary challenge to the violence of overwork.[53]

Many of us, in our desperate drive to be successful and care for our many responsibilities, feel terrible guilt when we take time to rest. If you are running out of time, you are either doing too much or doing what you do poorly. Kraft writes,

> John 15 is a great chapter on abiding in Christ. There is a deep and constant longing in my heart to experience genuine, intimate dependency on God on an ongoing basis. I get so tired so fast and stay tired longer when I fall into the trap of believing it's all up to me.[54]

Just because you *can*, doesn't mean you *should*. So many competent leaders have a plethora of diverse skills. They are *good* at almost everything. Because they can do so much, they do too much. Like a multi-function pocketknife, they can be utilized for anything—in which case they are never really *great* at anything.

13
CHILD

Life Script #2: "I am a child of God, loved by the Father."

"Behold what manner of love the Father hath bestowed upon us,
that we should be called children of God"

(1 John 3:1, ASV).

My three sons are still young and I have no idea what their careers will be, nor do I know whom they will marry. I do not know if they will make good decisions or bad ones. I pray they will make positive contributions to their community, but they may not. They may be successful, or prone to failure. In any case, my love level for them will always remain constant. Nothing they do can alter that love. The entire world may despise them, but as a father my love will stay steady. Their achievements, or lack thereof, will not impact that love level.

The great truth is that God thinks the same of you. When Jesus was water baptized by John, He came up out of the water and a voice said, *"This is my Son, whom I love; with him I am well pleased."* (Matthew 3:17). Jesus, at that point, had not completed a single earthly ministry task. God's love pre-exists your performance and remains constant throughout your journey. If you cannot embrace this script, you will work for love rather than from the certainty that you are loved. You cannot know the security of God through intelligence alone, because you are not clever enough, but even a kid can know Him through the heart.

I recently spoke at a leadership retreat for Bible college students. We were discussing the need to be able to trust God in order to achieve successful ministry. As we neared the end and began to pray, a young student began to weep. After a few minutes, she explained that she found it impossible to trust God. She was scared of what He might require of her and whether or not that level of commitment might be too painful or sacrificial.

She was expressing feelings all of us shared. We are all concerned about what following God might mean for us. We fear that God might see harm done to us because we feel He doesn't truly love us like He does others. There are a lot of people who say, "God loves you," but are unable to say, "God loves me." What a sad situation.

If you don't know who you are in Christ, you'll spend your entire life trying to prove who you are to others. You must believe that God's love for you is not impacted by the quantity of sin in your life, nor by your performance as a leader. You cannot judge yourself, or God's affection for you, based on the outcome of your efforts.

14
CHOSEN

Life Script #3: "I am chosen and called."

God has placed you where you are; rest in that. A script like this anchors and grounds us so we become stable, unshakable, and resolved.

Several years ago, I led a team into Romania. I was excited about the trip and was certain that we would be able to make a solid dent in the needs of that country. Communism fell in 1989 and the country struggled to find its feet in a political system that, although free, left a lot of uncertainty concerning much of the society's operation. I knew our team would be able to accomplish a lot. However, by the third day I was annoyed at everything—the country, the team, and myself. We awoke to another day of trips to the orphanage. The students loved the work in the orphanages, but it made me a little stir-crazy. I resigned myself to sitting on a chair and completing some paperwork while the team cared for the kids.

At one point, I found myself alone and still irritated at our lack of effectiveness. I noticed a door into a room we had not been allowed to enter. (All the doors and windows in Romania are frequently shut because of a superstition that sickness and evil can be carried by a gust or draft.) While everyone was outside in the playground, workers included, I decided to explore.

I entered the room to see three cribs, each with a toddler lying on the mattresses. It was sweltering, stinky, and sticky. (Diaper changes were restricted to once or twice per day.) These children had mental or physical deformities. I presumed they weren't allowed to interact like the other children now playing in the yard.

As I stepped deeper into the room the children saw me and their wide eyes spoke of their apprehension about this oversized intruder in their private room. To break the ice, I leaned over the first crib and tummy-tickled the first toddler. The reaction I got told me that he had never been tickled before. His scream threatened to get me busted, so I moved on to the second crib. Same tactic. Same result.

By now, the third kid was standing to catch a view of the strange white monster. I looked over and said, "You wanna piece of this?" With that, I stepped up to the third crib and tickled him incessantly. It took a few minutes, but they soon learned this new game and didn't want it to end. When I tickled one toddler, the others would start crying until I tickled them as well. For fifteen minutes I hustled from crib to crib trying to keep them all primed with tickles. I felt like one of those circus performers trying to spin glass plates on the end of sticks.

Tickling became exhausting, especially in that hot and humid room, but I couldn't stop. I couldn't leave a child untickled, especially when they had never been tickled before. I couldn't pull myself away from the cribs knowing that this might be their last tickle. Soon I heard the sound of students returning and I was forced to make an exit. As I put my hand on the door handle and looked back at three kids standing up in their beds wanting more, I began to feel that gentle rebuke of the Spirit: "Jim, that's all I wanted you to do today. Simply tickle a few babies."

I don't always like the answer when I ask myself the question, "Why do you want success?"

Do things because they matter to God, not because they get you noticed. He has called you. You must obey, no matter what the call, whether grandiose or trivial. Mother Teresa said, "I don't do big things. I do small things with big love." We all look for big things to do, but Jesus took the towel and washed the disciples' feet, for that was his calling; it became the primary metaphor for Christian faith. *"See to it that you complete the work you have received in the Lord"* (Colossians 4:17). *"[You] are God's workmanship, created in Christ Jesus to do good works"* (Ephesians 2:10).

We have been called to obedience, not merely accomplishment. Obey the call. You will gain security.

15
AUDIENCE

Life Script #4: "God is the audience of my life."

It is almost impossible for us to not lend an ear to the words of dissatisfaction or the nods of approval from those who observe our leadership. But under Christ we have nothing to prove, nothing to gain, and nothing to lose. If God is smiling on you, then neither the smile nor frown of man can affect you. "Be who you are and say what you feel because those who mind don't matter and those who matter don't mind."[55] Our unhealthy striving might be the result of poor theology, for if we truly believe we are saved by grace, we would stop trying so hard to amaze everyone with our performance.

Os Guinness writes, "Most of us, whether we are aware of it or not, do things with an eye to the approval of some audience or other. The question is not whether we have an audience, but which audience we have."[56] When others become our audience, we become susceptible to manipulation and control. People begin to have control over us. Those in our inner circle can unwittingly take advantage of us. This always leads to resentment.

David Kraft writes:

> When are we going to wake up and deal with ego and insecurity and humbly take roles that God intended for us, rather than those

we desire for the wrong reasons? If you are in leadership and feel frustrated, or if you are thinking about taking on a leadership role, I urge you to take an honest look at your gifting, experience, and passion. Listen clearly to what others are saying. Ascertain whether you have a leadership role to play and have the God-given abilities to carry it out. There's too much at stake to take leadership lightly and step into it for glory, applause, power, attention, or monetary rewards.[57]

The public ministry of John the Baptist lasted perhaps six months, but what was Jesus' estimate of John's life? *"I tell you, among those born of women there is no one greater than John"* (Luke 7:28). His life is a demonstration of the power of working for an audience of one.

A worthwhile exercise for me to do occasionally is to complete the statements below. They help remind me of my identity in Christ and serve to realign my perspective. Take a moment to try to complete a few of these.

I do not have to _____.

I do not have to _____.

I do not have to _____.

I am not _____.

I am not _____.

I am not _____.

16

SELF-AWARE

Life Script #5: "I know myself."

My son Jake and I were out for a ride on our all-terrain vehicles one Sunday afternoon. We like to take along our GPS, mark where we park the car, and then go exploring. To get back to base when we are finished we just switch on the GPS and its digital needle points the way. On one occasion the batteries had run low, but the GPS still knew where the car was parked. The problem was, it was telling us we were located in the Atlantic Ocean just off the coast of Europe. Some leaders today know where they want to go and have a basic understanding of how to get there, but they have little clue where they are.

William Glasser wrote, in *Reality Therapy*,

> If we do not evaluate our own behavior, or having evaluated it, we do not act to improve our conduct where it is below our standards, we will not fulfill our need to be worthwhile and we will suffer as acutely as when we fail to love or be loved. Morals, standards, values, or right and wrong behavior are all intimately related to the fulfillment of our need for self-worth.[58]

Ben Franklin said, "There are three things extremely hard: Steel, a diamond, and to know oneself." Personality tests, skill assessments, gift inventories, and countless books help us today to understand ourselves. Use them! Just remember to temper them with an understanding of the call of God on our life. While our behaviour is mostly a reflection of our beliefs about who we are, and we perform according to this self-perception, we must seek to know what the Word says of us. Here is what the Bible says of YOU:

- You are a child of God. (John 1:12, paraphrased)

- You are Christ's friend. (John 15:15, paraphrased)

- You are chosen and appointed by Christ to bear fruit. (John 15:16, paraphrased)

- You are a son/daughter of God. (Romans 8:14–15, paraphrased)

- You are a part of His family. (Romans 8:16, paraphrased)

- You are a joint heir with Christ, sharing His inheritance with Him. (Romans 8:17, paraphrased)

- You are joined (united) to the Lord and you are one spirit with Him. (1 Corinthians 6:17, paraphrased)

- You are a part of Christ's body. (1 Corinthians 12:27, paragraphed; see also Ephesians 5:30)

- You are reconciled to God and are a minister of reconciliation. (2 Corinthians 5:18–19, paraphrased)

- You are a son/daughter of God and one in Christ. (Galatians 3:26, 28, paraphrased)

- You are an heir of God, since you are a son/daughter of God. (Galatians 4:6–7, paraphrased)

- You are a saint. (Ephesians 1:1, paraphrased; see also 1 Corinthians 1:2, Philippians 1:1, and Colossians 1:2)

- You are a fellow citizen with the rest of God's the people in God's family. (Ephesians 2:19, paraphrased)

- You are hidden with Christ in God. (Colossians 3:3, paraphrased)

- You are an expression of the life of Christ because He is your life. (Colossians 3:4, paraphrased)

- You are chosen of God, holy, and dearly loved. (Colossians 3:12, paraphrased)

- You are selected and deeply loved by God. (1 Thessalonians 1:4, paraphrased)

- You are a son/daughter of light and not of darkness. (1 Thessalonians 5:5, paraphrased)

- You are a holy brother/sister, a partaker of a heavenly calling. (Hebrews 3:1, paraphrased)

- As a Christian, you are a part of a chosen race, a royal priesthood, a holy nation, a people for God's own possession to proclaim the excellencies of Him. (1 Peter 2:9–10, paraphrased)

- You are now a child of God. You will resemble Christ when He returns. (1 John 3:1–2, paraphrased)

- You are born of God; the evil one (the devil) cannot touch you. (1 John 5:18, paraphrased)

Emotional self-awareness is vital. Even if we are operating anywhere near our potential, an occasional wave of insecurity is inevitable. In fact, an occasional tidal wave is predictable. The lack of awareness of those emotions, and/or the denial of them, is what traps leaders. If such emotions remain unnoticed and unacknowledged, they will inevitably infect our thought and decision-making processes.

Everyone has emotional needs. Some leaders deny having them, which is a denial of their humanness. Others demand that their emotional needs always be in the forefront, and they care only about their own needs. They disregard the needs of others. Both of these damage psychological health and security. This is why so much is being written now about the leadership skill of emotional self-awareness, or "emotional intelligence." It is this awareness that clears the way for choice, wisdom, and creativity. Unacknowledged emotion loads our internal airwaves with static. To stop defeating ourselves, we must stop deceiving ourselves. Is there anything in your life you are pretending isn't a problem ?

The quest for self-awareness must be tempered with grace and optimism. Andrew Carnagie said, "Finding greatness in an individual is a lot like mining for gold. When you go into the mine you realize that you will have to move a ton of dirt to find an ounce of gold. However, you never go to the mine looking for the dirt. You always go to the mine looking for the gold!" If you go looking for dirt you will find plenty of it. But if you look *through* the dirt, you will find elements of yourself of real value.

Awareness must be accompanied by gentle acceptance. The emotions triggered in us are programmed early and deeply. Our automatic emotional responses are determined at a very early age. Recent research indicates that as much as ninety percent of our automatic responses are set by the age of five. So judging ourselves for certain emotions—or engaging in an effort to eradicate, root out, and crush those emotion—is, in itself, anxiety-provoking. Thus the first helpful response to anxiety is an acceptance of its occurrence. Calm response allows the more debilitating emotions to dissipate. By contrast, efforts to suppress them actually strengthen their power over our thinking.

We lack self-awareness for a few reasons. It may be because we have no sources of feedback in our lives. This points to our need of mentors, seasoned leaders, and older believers. If you don't get much feedback on your life and leadership, I suggest you get married; nothing makes you more aware of yourself! I was perfect until I got married. I never realized how selfish I was.

We are also unaware because we do not take the time to examine ourselves. We are too busy or distracted to take the time to reflect. Effective leaders are students of their own behaviours and emotions. Therefore, leaders need a lot more mirrors than windows in their lives, particularly when things are not going well. We must not look out the window for someone else to blame without first considering the reflection of our own culpability.

In particular, leaders must know about pressure. What are the trigger points? How do I know when I am stressed? What are the effects of stress? Below is a series of questions that may help you. Jot down your answers as you make discoveries:

- What happens to your spiritual life and disciplines when you are stressed?

- What sins are you more prone to indulge in when you are tired or stressed?

- Does stress seem to target a specific part of your body? If so, which part?

- What happens to your relationships when you are stressed? Do you have time for them? Do you spend time with others and not your key relationships?

- How do you know when you are physically worn out? What are the signs?

- When you are stressed, what do you do with your feelings? Do you bury your emotions? Do you "wear them on your sleeve?"

- How do you spend your time? Do you run to the television or a video game? What is the best way for you to unwind?

- How do you treat those in need when you are stressed?

- What happens to your brain during tough seasons? Do you get bored or apathetic? Do you need to stimulate with more caffeine?

Personality Assessment Tools

There are plenty of resources to help you determine your personality type. Access these tools to discover the tendencies of your particular temperament. They are very helpful in resolving insecurity through enhancing personal understanding.

The *16PF Questionnaire* was developed by Raymond Cattell and his colleagues in the 1940s and 1950s in a search to discover the basic traits of human personality using scientific methodology. The test was first published in 1949 and is now in its fifth edition, published in 1994. It is used in a wide variety of settings for individual and marital counselling, career counselling, and employee development—both in educational settings and for basic research.

My favourite is *Myers-Briggs Type Indicator*, which was developed during World War II by Isabel Myers and Katherine Briggs.

Another good test is the *Birkman*. In summary, The Birkman method includes five major perspectives: 1. Usual Behavior - an individual's effective behavioral style of dealing with relationships and tasks. 2. Underlying Needs - an individual's expectations of how relationships and social situations should be governed in context of the relationship or situation. 3. Stress Behaviors - an individual's ineffective style of dealing with relationships or tasks; behavior observed when underlying needs are not met. 4. Interests - an individual's expressed preference for job titles based on the assumption of equal economic rewards. 5. Organizational Focus - the perspective in which an individual views problems and solutions relating to organizational goals.

For a quick and easy test, I have used the *DISC* personality test. It is the four-quadrant behavioural model based on the work of Dr. William Moulton Marston (1893–1947). It focuses on styles and preferences.

17
MISSION

Life Script #6: "I know why I'm here and what I'm supposed to do."

> There are many people who think they want to be matadors, only to find themselves with 2000 pounds of bull bearing down on them, and then discover that what they really wanted was to wear tight pants and hear the crowd roar.[59]

What am I here for? Who am I? What have I been made to do? Do you know what you must get done and what you must leave undone? A *USA Today* poll in September 2006 found that if most people were given the opportunity to ask God one question, it would be: "What is my purpose in life?"

If your vision of leadership is too nebulous, insecurity is inevitable. My soul resonates with Soren Kierkegaard: "What I really lack is to be clear in my mind what I am to do, not what I am to know… The thing is to understand myself, to see what God really wishes me to do… to find the idea for which I can live and die."

Solving the mystery of "personal vision" is a cornerstone for achieving confidence and security. We have the opportunity to end up somewhere on purpose if we have the faith to attempt to see it. Someone said to Mike Vance, director of Disney Studios, "Isn't it too bad that Walt Disney didn't live to see this?" Vance answered, "He did see it; that's why it's here."

One characteristic of Jesus was that He knew His personal mission and wasn't distracted from it. When crowds gather before us, we are pulled toward them, but Jesus was often seen pulling away from them: *"Now when he saw the crowds, he went up on a mountainside and sat down"* (Matthew 5:1). We are guilty of thinking that just because we can do something, we should do something. If you did all the things you could do, you would drive yourself crazy. We have to lead by faith, and not by sight. If we respond to every need or opportunity we see, we may completely miss that which we were meant to do.

We are not to *create* a mission; we *receive* a mission. For spiritual leaders in particular, we must lead by *revelation*, not just *reason*. Leadership is more responsive than creative. Spiritual leadership is finding God's plan and getting people into it. Even Jesus didn't know the Father's full plan; He just remained obedient. In Matthew 24:36–37, Jesus admits, *"No one knows about that day or hour, not even the angels in heaven, nor the Son, but only the Father. As it was in the days of Noah, so it will be at the coming of the Son of Man."* Other times, we see Jesus affirming, *"The Son can do nothing by himself; he can only do what he sees his Father doing"* (John 5:19).

Jesus had a mission, but no play-by-play agenda. He just did what the Father said. He didn't heal everyone. He didn't speak to every crowd or accept every invitation. He wasn't even fond of the Cross idea, as we see in Matthew 26:39 – *"Going a little farther, he fell with his face to the ground and prayed, 'My Father, if it is possible, may this cup be taken from me. Yet not as I will, but as you will"* (Matthew 26:39). A little later, He prays again, *"My Father, if it is not possible for this cup to be taken away unless I drink it, may your will be done."* (Matthew 25:42). And again: *"So he left them and went away once more and prayed the third time, saying the same thing."* (Matthew 25:44). The leader's mantra must be: "Not as I will, but as You will."

Below are some steps to finding your personal mission. It might not be as dramatic as Peter's: *Upon this rock I will build my church*, or *Feed my sheep*; or even James', *I will make you a fisher of men*, but you have a God-given mission, and you can have certainty about it. For a leader, if one fails to get this block in place, the entire structure will topple. A sense of mission is key to security. Too many leaders bounce down the road, curb to curb, hoping to end up somewhere where they can claim they have ended up on purpose. It is like the proverbial shooting of the arrow and running ahead to place the target to ensure a bull's-eye. They remind me of Lewis Carroll's, *Alice in Wonderland*:

> "Would you tell me, please, which way I ought to go from here?"
> "That depends a good deal on where you want to get to," said the Cat.
> "I don't much care where," said Alice.
> "Then it doesn't much matter which way you go," said the Cat.
> "So long as I get somewhere," Alice added as an explanation.
> "Oh, you're sure to do that," said the Cat, "if only you walk long enough."[60]

Living mostly in your "sweet spot" will breed confidence. The sweet spot is actualized when a person operates at the center of his or her skill, knowledge, talent, and gifts, reaches full ministry strength, and lives in empowerment. A skill is something acquired through training over a period of time (such as typing). Knowledge is something you learn (such as knowing that if you kick a wasp nest, you will get stung). A talent is a natural aptitude for something which is developed and formed over time (such as playing the piano). A gift is given by God beyond one's natural ability and is always given as "ours for others" (such as serving). All of these can only be discovered by *"doing,"* not *"hearing."* **The only way to learn to lead is by leading**. You find your *calling* by examining your *gifts*, but only determine your *gifts* by *serving others*.

There are some clues as to what your "sweet spot" might be. Certainly skills, knowledge, talents, and gifts are primary clues. The biggest clue, however, is that which God speaks to your heart, that thing which is embedded in your soul. For me, the guidance counsellor's tests told me to stay away from most of the things I do now. When God postured me toward leadership, I was terrified. I did not have people skills, intellectual skills, or public speaking abilities. I would fake sick during school days when public presentations were required of me. Miraculously, and I mean *miraculously*, I have now spoken to thousands and lead in some great organizations. Whenever I take the platform, I smirk inside (and sometimes outside), because I know that this is not naturally who I am. It is supernatural. God is making up the difference!

So listen to the voice of the Spirit and mix in your competencies, history, disabilities, likes, and dislikes. Add in your family situation, networks of friends, and the realities at hand and you will discover your "sweet spot." Remember, we find our groove more easily by ruling out the things we aren't, so do not be afraid to try new things on for size.

Isaiah Berlin's essay, "The Hedgehog and the Fox," is a good illustration of focused vision. Many writers have used the essay as a metaphor for several leadership traits. For example, the historian Joseph Ellis uses the "Hedgehog and Fox" concept in evaluating George Washington, noting, "George Washington was an archetypal hedgehog. And the one big thing he knew was that America's future as a nation lay to the West, in its development over the next century of a continental empire," which was one of the reasons, according to Ellis, that Washington was devoted to the construction of canals.[61]

The story depicts how people approach problems differently. Some people are like foxes, knowing many things. Others are like hedgehogs, because they know one main thing. A fox is a smart animal able to develop many strategies for attacking the hedgehog. Like the cartoon Wile E. Coyote, the fox looks like he has another foolproof plan to finally catch his prey. The hedgehog, however, is a slow and dull animal whose defence is the same no matter how the fox attacks. Every day the fox thinks he is in for a tasty lunch, but no matter what the fox does, the hedgehog again rolls up into a little ball, spreads his sharp spikes, and thwarts the fox's plans.

Berlin explained that some people (foxes) see the world in all its complexity. Their approach constantly changes depending on the circumstances, but *they never develop a unified vision*. Other people (hedgehogs), on the other hand, simplify the complexity of the world into one principle—one basic idea that determines their every move. Hedgehogs are not stupid. Actually, their understanding of the world is so insightful that they're able to recognize the most basic principle of life.

Every leader has problems, concerns, and obstacles in his or her leadership. Some challenges may even be acute, but you do not need a new solution for every problem. Be a hedgehog, not a fox, because for a hedgehog the solution is always the same! When your vision/mission is resolved, it becomes the essential point of reference for what your next steps will be, what you will do, or what you won't do. You begin to operate by that value. If you do not know what you are meant to do, you will do many things without meaning.

Once you think you have identified your mission, test it. Is it based solely on your ego? Does it change people's lives? Is it big enough to require dependence on God? Does it mean you will have to be a servant? Have others confirmed it to you? Will it require you to be great in character? How will you feel if you don't do it? Are you "seeking first the Kingdom?"

Now, do it! There is the danger of just thinking. Sometimes the fact that we thought of doing something new makes us feel that we have done something new. I once heard someone say that there are those that "think old, do old" and some who "think new, do new." But then there is a deceived crowd that "think new, do old." Vision and implementation are of equal importance.

I once wrote this personal statement: "I am a stagehand, just a crew member. I prepare the platform, but if He doesn't show up, there is nothing to see. I am not the main act. I am not in the crowd, either. I'm not even a stage-manager—that's someone else's job. I'm backstage. I will be faithful, but mostly unseen." I know this means little to you. It is not profound, but it gave me a sense of being "put in my place."

18

SELF-DISCIPLINE

Life Script #7: "I am disciplined and self-controlled."

When it comes to "spiritual disciplines," we have made our spiritual lives mechanical and formulaic—sort of a "punch-clock" relationship. It doesn't work in marriage or friendships, so it is not going to work in spiritual life. Spiritual discipline isn't about trying harder or earning merit points. Such things are the poison of legalists. Someone once said, "To be like Jesus we need to practice the habits of Jesus." Godly living doesn't just happen. We must work at it if we are to have a spiritual maturity equal to our ministry.

How many spiritual disciplines are there? We usually name two: prayer and Bible reading. Some may add fasting. There are actually plenty more, and the practice of them boosts our confidence and lowers insecurity levels.

Of course, prayer and meditation have the greatest effect on our sense of belonging to God and our ability to trust that our lives are divinely influenced and directed. This is why Paul writes in Philippians 4:6, *"Do not be anxious about anything, but in everything, by prayer and petition, with thanksgiving, present your requests to God."* In Colossians 4:2 he says, *"Devote yourselves to prayer, being watchful and thankful."* And in 1 Thessalonians 5:16–18 he writes,

"Be joyful always; pray continually; give thanks in all circumstances, for this is God's will for you in Christ Jesus."

The full scope of a disciplined life includes fasting, Bible study, regular confession of sins and faults, rejoicing, solitude, silence, submission to authority, works of service, singing, worship, and sustaining healthy relationships.

A few years ago, I assessed my own failings in spiritual disciplines and tried to articulate some core reasons why I was unfaithful and lazy in this regard. Apart from life's busyness (work, marriage, children, illnesses, hobbies), I realized that I had some hefty core problems. I was living like "as though *doing*" things for Jesus outweighed just *being* with Jesus. I subconsciously convinced myself that I did not have time. But like Bill Hybels said, "If you are too busy to pray, you are too busy." Deeper than that, for me, was a faith issue: I didn't really believe that practicing spiritual disciplines would change anything. I was not convinced that it actually made a difference. My heart knew better, but my head was in doubt.

The authors of *The Leader's Journey* write:

> Spiritual disciplines are the means by which these automatic reactions are ultimately changed. The disciplines work to rewire our automatic reaction, offering us options about how to respond in a given situation. We no longer have to react as we once did. In fact, practicing the spiritual disciplines helps us see ourselves and the rest of the system with clarity and divinely guided insight so that we can make our choice on the basis of God's revealed truth rather than from the pressures brought to bear on us by the system.[62]

19
TRANSPARENT

Life Script #8: "Others have right of access into my life."

Insecurity likes to live in our blind spots. Because insecurity is so sneaky, we need feedback from friends. A few days ago, a good friend who is a "know-it-all" accused me of also being a "know-it-all." I was annoyed. Like the sign says, "Those who think they know it all are really annoying to those of us who do!" I'm joking. Regardless, good feedback is golden. The challenging questions asked by friends and colleagues are priceless. Great leaders have sounding boards.

- Who asks you the tough and probing questions?
- Who knows how to call your "bluff?"
- Who gets you thinking?
- Who tells you off when you are out of line?
- Who has the permission to be honest with you?

Several years ago, a famous evangelist was exposed for a moral failure. A full-blown scandal erupted. When the fanfare died down, the former evangelist was asked why he hadn't spoken to someone about the struggle he was having. This man, known by millions, answered, "Because I had no one to talk to." Therein was the real tragedy: his life lived in the midst of a crowd, was also lived in isolation.

There is a reason why Scripture admonishes us to be quick to announce our failures, faults, and shortcomings to our brothers and sisters in Christ. Without confession, our lives are destined for defeat. If a leader has no one to whom to answer, they will fail to have protected themselves in all areas of their life and leadership.

Submission is difficult for those who are insecure first because it allows others to highlight the things that aggravate their insecurity in the first place. It challenges their self-esteem and sense of control, and triggers their paranoia. Secondly, submission requires vulnerability. Vulnerability is the perceived enemy of insecurity. It causes insecure leaders to be withdrawn and emotionally reclusive.

If no one is permitted to have passage into your life, you are either obnoxious or insecure. You will mistakenly think you have it all together, or you will feel like your life has a propensity to be in shambles.

20
OTHERS

"When Christ calls a man, he bids him come and die."

(Dietrich Bonhoeffer)

Life Script #9: "I serve the King by serving others."

Hobbes: "Whatcha doin'?"

Calvin: "Getting rich!"

Hobbes: "Really?"

Calvin: "Yep. I'm writing a self-help book! There's a huge market for this stuff. First, you convince people there's something wrong with them. That's easy, because advertising has already conditioned people to feel insecure about their weight, looks, social status, sex appeal, and so on. Next, you convince them that the problem is not their fault and that they're victims of larger forces. That's easy, because it's what people believe anyway. Nobody wants to be responsible for his own situation. Finally, you convince them that with your expert advice and encouragement, they can conquer their problem and be happy!"

Hobbes: "Ingenious. What problem will you help people solve?"

Calvin: "Their addiction to self-help books! My book is called, 'Shut up and Stop Whining: How to Do Something with Your Life Besides Think About Yourself.'"

Hobbes: "You should probably wait for the advance before buying anything."

Calvin: "The trouble is… if my program works, I won't be able to write a sequel."[63]

There is an enormous market for "self-help" resources today. However, "self-help" can become "self-absorbed." One of the best ways to beat self-centeredness, and thus insecurity, is to learn to serve. During one of the darker moments in my soul, I came across this verse: *"If you spend yourselves in behalf of the hungry and satisfy the needs of the oppressed, then your light will rise in the darkness, and your night will become like the noonday"* (Isaiah 58:10). It motivated me to get off my butt and look for ways to brighten someone else's life. As I did, light began to shine inside my soul, warming my inner being and removing discouragement.

Every now and then, we forget why we do what we do or, more importantly, for whom we do it. It's not that we actually forget, but we become numb to that acute awareness that responsibility requires. Every leader lives through seasons of complacency. It just happens. The business and busyness of leading causes us to lead out of ritual and routine. Peoplework gets upstaged by paperwork. The important gives way to the urgent. Sometimes demands and duties can even make for an excuse to disengage. We start to view people as interruptions. But frankly, people do not want to follow anyone who doesn't care about them. Treat people as if they are already what they ought to be and they will be motivated to become what they are capable of being. Relationships do not fit our deadline mentality, but relationships are the point. In the end, we will be rewarded by what we have done and, more importantly, how we served in the lives of others. Albert Schweitzer said, "One thing I know: the only ones among you who will be really happy are those who will have sought and found how to serve."

On another outdoor adventure, I was riding our four-wheel ATV and Jake was riding his dirt bike. We weren't lost; we prefer the term "exploring." We were further away from the car than I thought and night was creeping up on us. By the time we came to within a couple kilometres of the car, it was dark. My machine had a headlight, but Jake's did not. It is not easy driving through the forest in the dark; in fact, it is impossible. To get home, we positioned a friend, Kevin, in front of Jake, and I rode behind him. Jake kept following Kevin's taillights while I lit his path from behind. We made it back safely.

That is an appropriate picture of what leaders are to be for others. Even if you are insecure, become preoccupied with lighting someone else's way and you will soon forget your own concerns. Lead someone, or at least light his or her life, with hope. This is an important principle for combating insecurity. Be an encourager and you will not be insecure. Insecurity and encouragement mix like oil and water.

Mother Teresa was a modern day servant who lived almost exclusively for others. One of her most memorable quotes was, "Don't look for big things, just do small things with great love... The smaller the thing, the greater must be our love."[64] She considered herself just "a pencil in God's hand" and was convinced that God was using her "nothingness" to show His greatness. What great theology! Another of my favourite expressions of hers was, "Be kind to each other—I prefer you make mistakes in kindness than that you work miracles in unkindness."[65] One nun told a story of a visit by Mother Teresa: "After we had lunch, Mother helped us to wash the dishes and she was the first one to take the dishcloth to clean off the table. People were crowded outside because of Mother, and here Mother is doing the humblest act like a simple sister."[66]

Although it is inevitable, being a servant doesn't mean being taken advantage of by others. I once heard someone say that being a servant doesn't mean we become a doormat; it means we become a doorway. Blackaby writes, "Being God's servant is quite different from working for a human master. While an ordinary servant labors *for* his master, God works *through* His servants."[67]

Matthew 20 contains the most pointed example of Christ's paradigm shift for the leaders of his day. It is one of his "not so with you" phrases:

> Jesus called them together and said, "You know that the rulers of the Gentiles lord it over them, and their high officials exercise authority over them. Not so with you. Instead, whoever wants to become great among you must be your servant, and whoever wants to be first must be your slave—just as the Son of Man did not come to be served, but to serve, and to give his life as a ransom for many. (Matthew 20:25–28)

People thrive on encouragement, affirmation, and praise. We underestimate the impact of a tiny amount of touch, kindness, or affirmation. What is your understanding of these scriptures below? Jot some notes to yourself. There are some keys to beating insecurity in each of them.

> James 1:19 – "Everyone should be quick to listen, slow to speak and slow to become angry." (James 1:19)

> Romans 12:15 – "Rejoice with those who rejoice; mourn with those who mourn." (Romans 12:15)

> 2 Corinthians 1:3-4 – "Praise be to the God and Father of our Lord Jesus Christ, the Father of compassion and the God of all comfort, who comforts us in all our troubles, so that we can comfort those in any trouble with the comfort we ourselves have received from God." (2 Corinthians 1:3–4)

> Galatians 6:2 – "Carry each other's burdens, and in this way you will fulfill the law of Christ." (Galatians 6:2)

The truth is, you need people, and they need you. We were meant to live in community and the giving and receiving of service in community increases self-worth and self-esteem. This is especially true of leaders who have the proclivity to "go solo" so easily. Consider Rudyard Kipling's, "The Law of the Jungle":

> *Now this is the Law of the Jungle—*
> *as old and as true as the sky;*
> *And the Wolf that shall keep it may prosper,*
> *but the Wolf that shall break it must die.*
> *As the creeper that girdles the tree—*
> *trunk the Law runneth forward and back—*
> *For the strength of the Pack is the Wolf,*
> *and the strength of the Wolf is the Pack!*[68]

21

PRIVILEGE

Life Script #10: "I am blessed because God's not fair."

My first paycheque as a leader was supposed to be for $326.93 for one week's work. I arrived at my new post on Monday, set up my office, attended a day and a half of our District Conference, and then drove to my parents' house (five hours away) to pick up some belongings. I made it back in time to spend Saturday getting ready for my first Sunday. My first check was handed to me and it recorded: $326.93 x 4/7 = $186.82. The numbers may be off a bit, but I was discounted by three days' worth of work. Welcome to ministry leadership! Thankfully, I have written a book on insecurity that is sure to sell at least a dozen copies—my financially challenged days are over!

There is a mind-bending parable found in Matthew 20:

> For the kingdom of heaven is like a landowner who went out early
> in the morning to hire men to work in his vineyard. He agreed to
> pay them a denarius for the day and sent them into his vineyard.

About the third hour he went out and saw others standing in the marketplace doing nothing. He told them, "You also go and work in my vineyard, and I will pay you whatever is right."

He went out again about the sixth hour and the ninth hour and did the same thing. About the eleventh hour he went out and found still others standing around. He asked them, "'Why have you been standing here all day long doing nothing?'

"Because no one has hired us,'," they answered.

He said to them, "You also go and work in my vineyard."

When evening came, the owner of the vineyard said to his foreman, "'Call the workers and pay them their wages, beginning with the last ones hired and going on to the first."

The workers who were hired about the eleventh hour came and each received a denarius. So when those came who were hired first, they expected to receive more. But each one of them also received a denarius.

When they received it, they began to grumble against the landowner. "These men who were hired last worked only one hour," they said, "and you have made them equal to us who have borne the burden of the work and the heat of the day."

But he answered one of them, "'Friend, I am not being unfair to you. Didn't you agree to work for a denarius? Take your pay and go. I want to give the man who was hired last the same as I gave you. Don't I have the right to do what I want with my own money? Or are you envious because I am generous?' So the last will be first, and the first will be last."?"

So the last will be first, and the first will be last. (Matthew 20:1–16)

Somewhere along the way, we got "rights." Rights are probably a good thing, but I find it difficult to understand them against Paul's *"Though I am free... I make myself a slave to everyone,"* (1 Corinthians 9:19) or *"Be devoted to one another,"* or *"prefer one another."*[69] (Romans 12:10). We are concerned with fairness and recognition, but God seems to have a different economy.

I am glad God is not fair. The criminal on the cross, who only served Jesus for a few minutes, is glad that He is not fair. Thank God that *"He does not treat us as our sins deserve or repay us according to our iniquities"* (Psalm 103:10). If you only judge your worth by your measure of your economy, you will be insecure. In our thinking, we will never get paid enough, recognized enough, or treated right. But God sorts it out with His scales, not ours.

The one thing that the all-day worker got, over the other partial-day workers, was the "privilege" of working longer for the Master. It is not for personal "reward" or "profit" or "success" or the ability to state that we accomplished a big dream; it is about the privilege! The privilege *is* the reward. The criminal on the cross only served Jesus for a moment. We get to serve Him for a lifetime! The all-day worker received a call to serve, was permitted to be in the vineyard, and knew the landowner longer! Unlike others, he did not have to wait all morning wondering if he would be picked for work or be overlooked. It was not about what the worker did not get at the end of the shift; it was about what he got to miss. He did not need to feel the embarrassment of being unused. The Master chose him! George Bernard Shaw once wrote:

> This is the true joy in life, the being used for a purpose recognized by yourself as a mighty one; the being thoroughly worn out before you are thrown on the scrap heap; the being a force of nature instead of a feverish, selfish little clod of ailments and grievances complaining that the world will not devote itself to making you happy.[70]

In our Western culture, we face a crisis of "entitlement thinking." McDonald's once had a marketing theme that told us, "You deserve a break today." While sitting on our couch watching television all day, I learned not that I *needed* a break but that I *deserved* one. After all, I had been very busy doing nothing. What better way to reward myself then by heading out to clog a few more arteries? Thankfully, they had drive thru service, meaning I didn't have to make the strenuous trip from the car into the restaurant.

In the end, you and I received much more than we deserve so, *"whatever you do, work at it with all your heart, as working for the Lord, not for men."* (Colossians 3:23). I will bless the Lord at *all* times. It does not matter what we receive. What matters is what the Master receives.

"L'Envoi" by Rudyard Kipling

And only the Master shall praise us,
And only the Master shall blame;
And no one shall work for money,
And no one shall work for fame;
But each for the joy of the working,
And each in his separate star,
Shall draw the Thing as he sees
It for the God of the Things as They Are![71]

22

BONDAGE

Life Script #11: "I am free from the bondage of sin."

If you are in bondage to sin, you will feel like rubbish and be about as inse-cure as the third monkey trying to sneak on to Noah's Ark. You must there-fore take responsibility for your sin. It is yours. One of the funny quips I say to leaders is, "Own your own poo. You made it. Own it and deal with it." It is your responsibility.

Without repentance we cannot be secure. Repentance is a neglected biblical mandate. It doesn't sound appealing because it is not as attractive as talking about love or grace. Repentance, however, is an undeniable and essen-tial ingredient of the Gospel. Actually, it is the most fundamental component. *"Repent and be baptized."* (Acts 2:38). Notice that the word "repent" is the first word of the Gospel of Christ. Richard Owen Roberts writes, "One of the most shocking marks of our present moral and spiritual declension is that we also have forgotten how to blush!" He continues:

> Any prophet, priest, or preacher who claims to speak for God and says little or nothing about repentance in these desperately wicked days is certainly no spokesman for God, nor ought he to be trusted in other matters. True repentance does not stand alone but is always linked with true faith. True faith does not stand alone but

is always linked with true repentance. Both repentance and faith are mandatory to salvation. You must turn from your sin in order to turn to Jesus Christ. You cannot turn to Christ unless you have turned from your sin. Repentance and faith belong together.[72]

Temptations come to us one of three forms: money, sex, or power. These become more powerful with anonymity (online, in a hotel room, out of the country). Lord Nelson said, "Every sailor is a bachelor when beyond Gibraltar." And temptations are always more potent when you are stressed. Here are a couple of tips:

1. Do not ignore or bury your issues. Skeletons have a strange way of tumbling out of the closet.
2. Pay attention to the battles going on inside you.
3. Listen to the voice of your spouse and friends. If they are telling you that you are acting like an idiot, you *are* acting like an idiot.
4. Get a counsellor. Drop the ego. Be brave. Go get help.
5. Stick a thermometer on your pride levels (spouses and close friends are good for this, too).
6. Fight lust. Lust may be all the rage today, but it is still sin. If you look lustfully at a woman, it is as if you have slept with her.
7. Don't be lazy. Laziness causes sin. I don't know how. It just does.
8. Stay away from the love of money. If someone (or yourself) tries to convince you that you should cheat in order to get what you think you deserve, punch him in the nose. (While you're at it, if you meet a "prosperity gospel" preacher, punch him in the nose.)
9. If you need to be recognized, get more Facebook friends. Don't seek admiration from others.
10. Stop the habit of lying (often disguised as "exaggerating" or telling "white lies"). My wife told me a few years ago that I lied now and then. I told her that I never lie. I was lying. She was right. It made me mad.

23
STRESS

"Quietude, which some men cannot abide because it reveals their inward poverty, is as a palace of cedar to the wise, for along its hallowed courts the King in His beauty deigns to walk."

(Charles H. Spurgeon)

Life Script #12: "I am at ease."

As young boys, my friends and I spent almost all of our time playing in the woods. We would build tree forts and spend countless hours living in a make-believe world filled with fabricated adventures and daring missions.

One day, I was alone taking a trip into our new tree-fort construction project and passing through a large clearing. A couple hundred of yards away, I noticed a hunter in bright orange, carrying a rifle. He was far away, but I still could see him raise his gun and point it in my direction! I heard the crack of the first shot, and then a second, and I started running into thicker bush. To this day, I never knew why he shot at me. Likely I was mistaken for an animal, or maybe he'd had a few beers before hitting the trail. In any case, I was the target, so I ran flat-out into thick woods. Deeper and deeper I broke through the forest, full of panic and fright.

When I slowed to a walking pace, I was lost. In the commotion, I had lost my bearings. I continued a swift and disorganized walk. I was getting tired but was too focused (or too unfocused) to take a break. Finally, after hours of wandering meaninglessly, I stopped. I sat down. I rested. It only took a few moments of rest when I realized what I needed was a tall tree. A quick glance revealed the tallest tree and I scurried up the branches. From a new height, I could see that I was within a moderate walk from our town and in familiar woods. With new energy and proper direction, I headed toward home.

Sometimes what we need to do most is to do nothing. What we need is rest. It feels counterintuitive, because we believe we should be taking action! Rest will give you new energy and proper bearings. Insecure leaders push harder. Secure leaders know when to get out of the game for a break. It's like tobogganing as a child. There comes a point when the sled is going too fast and it is best to simply jump off. The trick is to get off while it is still possible. In his must-read book, *Leading On Empty*, Wayne Cordeiro writes:

> Your system has to recharge, but it requires a trickle charge, one that restores you with a sustained low-amperage. There is no quick return on this one. If you do this right, you may return to the level of ministry you had in the beginning. But honestly most never return to the level of performance they had before the burnout. If you can't take a year, take as long as you can. Any amount is better than nothing. The only way to finish strong will be to first replenish your system. If you don't, prepare for a crash.[73]

Stress is good. We need stress. It is by stress that we grow. It is not the *presence of stress* that destroys a leader; it is the *absence of rest*. In the sport's medicine world, this need of *stress and rest* is called *oscillation*. Athletes increase their capacity by stressing their bodies to the limit and then resting/refuelling their bodies. Jim Loehr, a performance psychologist, states:

> In the living laboratory of sports, we learned that the real enemy of high performance is not stress, which, paradoxical as it may seem, is actually the stimulus for growth. Rather, the problem is the absence of disciplined, intermittent recovery. Chronic stress without recovery depletes energy reserves, leads to burnout and breakdown, and ultimately undermines performance. Rituals that promote oscillation—rhythmic stress and recovery—are the sec-

ond component of high performance. Repeated regularly, these highly precise, consciously developed routines become automatic over time.[74]

For exercise, I swim in the mornings at a local pool. When I first started to swim, I expected to be able to perform like I did when I was a teen. Silly me. Halfway down the lane, I thought I was going to pass out! My body wasn't used to exercising like that. The next day, I could barely move. But time after time, swim after swim, I began to move past sore muscles and shortness of breath. I went from taking a full minute to complete a length, to fifty seconds, then forty seconds, and then thirty seconds. Sports scientists say that what I'm doing is damaging my muscles and letting them heal. This healing takes about forty-eight hours, and surprisingly my muscles have then become stronger. Conversely, when I fail to oscillate between stressing my muscles and resting, I send my muscles into atrophy.

If you are overstressed, it is more likely that you mean that you are under-rested. The stress is actually increasing your leadership ability—but only if you are permitting "oscillation." I doubt there is a formula for oscillation, because every person is different, but every person can optimize his or her stress and recovery pattern.

Take public speaking, for example. For North Americans, and likely in other countries, the number one fear is public speaking. (The second greatest fear is death. Therefore, as Jerry Seinfeld says, at a funeral the person having to give the eulogy would rather be the person in the box.) In order to become a great public speaker, you have to put yourself in the nervous place of being in front of a crowd, repeatedly. To have a better marriage, you have to have disagreements with your spouse. Often a child who is at odds with you only discovers the true depth of your love during times of crisis or discipline. Sometimes we need the stress of hitting rock-bottom before we are jolted enough to start to look upward.

Do you want to lead and be free of insecurity? If so, you must learn to rest effectively. Rest is a skill. Living in oscillation requires deliberate effort and hard work. Without rest, you cannot live or lead well. Musicians know that it's the space between notes that makes the music.

> You shall do no work at all... It is to be a sabbath of complete rest to you, and you shall humble your souls. (Leviticus 23:31–32, NASB)

24
COURAGE

Life Script #13: "I will not fear."

Sandy was raised in the remote northern Canadian town of Happy Valley, NL. When we first got married, access to Happy Valley was a three-day trip with a violent trek across a rough dirt road where few gas stations or amenities were available.

On our first trip to Sandy's home we completed the roughest part of the trip was dark, on a road that I had never driven before. On the way back, we drove the same road, but this time in daylight. Oddly, we made better time when we drove through the night. The difference was that at night I had no idea that I was driving along the edge of steep mountain cliffs, through tight ravines, and over narrow bridges. We moved a lot faster when I was completely unaware of the danger!

There is a narrow margin between bravery and stupidity. To be secure is not the same as being courageous, yet courage is a sign of security. I like Frank Starpoli's definition: "Courage can be understood as a willingness to act in concert with deeply held beliefs and values and vision, despite the emotional stirrings."

Courage is not a feeling, nor is courage simply a decision. It is a choice followed by an act. It is brave action, in spite of emotion, in the face of present, perceived, or potential threat. So courage is choice based on one's values and mission. It overcomes a fear and always results in action. For an action to be courageous it must naturally feel scary. Sometimes it will seem counterintuitive.

On the rough road to lessening insecurity, there are several "brave actions" to be tackled. What are areas of your life and leadership that require you to act courageously? To reduce insecurity, there are always scary obstacles to cross. Mostly, we must say farewell to the impression we hope others have of us. It may mean risking the image we have so industriously built for ourselves. Be warned. When we break from our proneness to respond with fear-based behaviour, there will always be sore and painful seasons of change. Some of the things we encounter are the very things we have been fearful of facing.

Uneasiness about how people will respond can be a source of emotional uncertainty. As I act courageously, will people think I am being arrogant? Will people stop liking me? Will my career/position be jeopardized? Will my primary relationships survive? Will there be anger, resistance, or other expressions of disappointment and resentment? Will the person I become be worse than who I am now?

The insecurities and fears that frequently prevent us from action are usually speculative and unrealistic. For example, the tough conversation we needed to have with a friend turns out to be "not so bad" and they appreciate our forthrightness. Last week I had to implement the difficult decision to eject a family from our non-profit summer camp. Their behaviour had certainly warranted the expulsion and one of their family members was a severe threat to the safety of other young campers. As expected, they were angry, but I had no choice. I was surprised to find an email in my inbox two days later expressing their gratitude for my concern for their family and the wellbeing of others. I feared losing respect, but the reverse was the outcome. Their respect for me actually increased as a result.

Brave Action #1: Doing what is right, regardless.

Yesterday, one of my closest friends emphatically insisted that I make a decision to issue a stern ultimatum to someone. For me, I knew it wasn't the right decision. A few others offered their opinion, in agreement with my friend, but it still didn't feel right. Within a few hours, I found myself with a position and decision that many disagreed with. Now, I believe in seeking the counsel of many, but in this case I didn't agree with the consensus. It was hard to do the opposite. I feared that people thought I was a coward, avoiding conflict. I was bothered by what people might say. I was worried about what people might do.

My desire to do what is right is too often impacted by what I fear people will think, what I fear people will say, and what I fear people will do. Those fears tempt me to compromise important values and prefer image over authenticity. They cause me to ignore reality about people and situations. They cause me to seek safety instead of truth. But I try to fight it. I am trying to live my life doing what is right, regardless.

We all know intimidation and what it feels like to bend to it. Everybody knows what it is like to feel these insecurities: scared of the consequences, worried about the potential loss, and fearful of how someone might react. Sometimes we tolerate the intolerable. Sometimes we excuse the inexcusable. Sometimes we become blind to the obvious. Sometimes we fail to lead. Yet it is always better to be detested for your courage than esteemed for following the crowd.

Brave Action #2: Taking leadership, regardless.

Most times in leadership it is impossible to figure out all the details before we have to act. Although leadership is not about command and control, the "buck stops" at the person in charge. For the insecure, there exists a temptation to hesitate to step up and provide the guidance that is expected from them. Taking leadership is often difficult for insecure people because they tend to confuse it with being proud or cocky. It tends to feel like one is acting in humility by not stepping up.

The other illusion is the need to "keep the peace." Some insecure leaders have a natural affinity for harmony and accord. Yet there are moments when harmony must be suspended in order for a ministry, organization, or individual to move forward. This is difficult for the insecure leader.

Brave Action #3: Facing off with people, regardless.

Insecure leaders do not handle conflict well. They are often prone to lash out, but they can also hermit themselves away to avoid interpersonal conflict.

Some pick fights and others will never fight—even if they should. Some never engage in crucial dialogue with people who are intimidating. They bypass hard conversations and their leadership effectiveness plummets.

Engaging conflict is an expected component of leadership. Without conflict, there cannot be leadership, nor can there be progress. We find it difficult to hold people accountable for their actions (or inaction). We fear angry responses and worry about hurting someone's feelings. We cower when we need to go toe-to-toe with colleagues or followers.

I am not suggesting we pick fights or be quick to confront. Proverbs 20:3 says, *"It is to a man's honor to avoid strife, but every fool is quick to quarrel."* When a clash is necessary, there are some scriptural principles for navigating through constructive conflict.

Take a moment to consider these verses, then jot a few notes in the space provided:

> *Proverbs 13:10* – "Pride only breeds quarrels, but wisdom is found in those who take advice."

> *Proverbs 17:14* – "Starting a quarrel is like breaching a dam; so drop the matter before a dispute breaks out."

> *Proverbs 19:11* – "A man's wisdom gives him patience; it is to his glory to overlook an offense."

> *Proverbs 20:18* – "Make plans by seeking advice; if you wage war, obtain guidance."

> *Proverbs 15:18* – "A hot-tempered man stirs up dissension, but a patient man calms a quarrel."

> *Proverbs 17:19* – "He who loves a quarrel loves sin; he who builds a high gate invites destruction."

Proverbs 18:2 – "A fool finds no pleasure in understanding but delights in airing his own opinions."

Proverbs 19:19 – "A hot-tempered man must pay the penalty; if you rescue him, you will have to do it again."

Proverbs 21:31 – "The horse is made ready for the day of battle, but victory rests with the LORD."

Proverbs 22:10 – "Drive out the mocker, and out goes strife; quarrels and insults are ended."

Proverbs 25:9 – "If you argue your case with a neighbour, do not betray another man's confidence."

Proverbs 25:21 – "If your enemy is hungry, give him food to eat; if he is thirsty, give him water to drink."

Proverbs 26:17 – "Like one who seizes a dog by the ears is a passer-by who meddles in a quarrel not his own."

Proverbs 26:20 – "Without wood a fire goes out; without gossip a quarrel dies down."

Proverbs 26:21 – "As charcoal to embers and as wood to fire, so is a quarrelsome man for kindling strife."

Proverbs 29:11 – "A fool gives full vent to his anger, but a wise man keeps himself under control."

The answer to managing conflict is maintaining "self-control." In fact, all of the other fruits of the Spirit (love, joy, peace, patience, kindness, goodness, faithfulness, and gentleness) are important in conflict, but self-control is vital.

Brave Action #4: Admitting ignorance, regardless.

"Never let 'em see you sweat" might be a great advertising slogan but is a stupid leadership strategy. Leaders who try to appear all-knowing and always-in-control are annoying. People don't respect them and usually don't like them. Followers get stubborn and close themselves off from this type of insecure leader. On the other hand, when a leader admits that he or she doesn't have the answer, they exhibit a commitment to an organization's advancement over personal image and clearly communicate value for people and the contributions they make. Leighton Ford wrote, "You see, we still didn't have it straight. We thought that the leader had to be totally in control. Or else, how could he be the leader? We were still blind to the fact that sometimes God works through your weakness, and not through strength."[75]

No leader knows it all, and when they pretend to, they create environments of anxiety, exhaustion, and frustration. The truth is, people intuitively know when you are faking it. Resentment follows. Compliance becomes half-hearted.

Weakness can actually be inspiring. According to Scripture, our strength is in our weakness. 2 Corinthians 3:5 says, *"Not that we are competent in ourselves to claim anything for ourselves, but our competence comes from God."* Those who evaluate us will judge not by how right we are, or how smart we are, or how grand and powerful we are, but by how much we serve those who are the least among us. To try to appear all-knowing and always-in-control is to make a statement about one's faith. That is, we don't have any.

Brave Action #5: Obeying the signals of our own tiredness, regardless.

Self-care is not selfish. It is, however, brave. Taking time to refresh yourself may not be understood by others. Very few will celebrate your vacation. Not many will tolerate your naps. There is a lot of lip service given with, "Remember to take care of yourself." It is courageous to practice self-care. It is scary to think that you may be thought of as lazy or slothful. The very people who tell me to "take care of myself" are the same ones who get upset when I don't answer their emails within an hour of receiving them. My colleague, Chris Falconer says, "'The devil doesn't take a vacation' is often heard, but I try to never use the devil as my example."

It is also brave to get professional help. A few years ago, I helped set up a program with a professional counselling service that would allow our leaders to have three complimentary anonymous counselling sessions with a professional counsellor. It worked well. Then someone suggested I should go. I hesitated. To be honest, I was uneasy with the idea. In the end, it was one of the best things I've done.

> When I am afraid, I will trust in you. In God, whose word I praise, in God I trust; I will not be afraid. What can mortal man do to me? (Psalm 56:3–4)

25

AMBITION

Life Script #14: "I am excited to live and lead."

There is a joke that every pastor has heard: "It must be great to be a pastor. You only have to work one day a week!" If you are a pastor, you know that's not true. If you're a pastor or other sort of leader, you know what it's like to try to juggle all the parts of life—including work, family, friends, faith, and community service.

A few years ago, *Time* featured this cover: "Ambition: Why Some People Are Most Likely To Succeed." The subtitle read, "A fire in the belly doesn't light itself. Does the spark of ambition lie in genes, family, culture—or even in your own hands? Science has answers." Authors cited successful leaders like Donald Trump, Bill Clinton, Oprah Winfrey, and Tiger Woods. Trump, they said, used to love to read the foreclosure listings in the newspaper. Bill Clinton, at age sixteen, defeated a thousand other boys in a mock campaign for a senate seat. Oprah was an early reader (age two) and fought to start in the first grade, then went on to skip into the third. At age six, Tiger Woods, the world's greatest golfer, was listening to motivational tapes.

So is it all genetics and personality type? The magazine never went on to answer those questions, but the questions were intriguing anyway. What determines a "go-getter" from a "do-nothing?" Why are there some couch-stuck inventors while others become successful entrepreneurs? Where does the inner drive come from?

The answer is "motivation."

Ambition always has a motivator. The leader must know what force gives him or her the strong desire to achieve something.

Ambition = energy + determination + goals

The apostle Paul was clear about his ambition. *"I have fully proclaimed the gospel of Christ. It has always been my ambition to preach the gospel where Christ was not known, so that I would not be building on someone else's foundation."* (Romans 15:19–20). His statement shares some common themes with other New Testament leaders. It is purposeful and full of godly effort. Creativity is cherished. Uncertainty is embraced. Security is abandoned. They possessed a trailblazing spirit which desired to take new ground, pioneer, or cut a new path. Today, before us is a leadership challenge: Matthew 9:37 says, *"The workers are few..."*

The Problem of Lack of Ambition

Hebrews 6:12 records, *"We do not want you to be lazy, but to imitate those who [have gone before]."*

There are lethargic leaders. For everyone working sixty hours per week, someone is punching out early every day. The next generation, in particular, has significant issues with ambition and achievement. I often get calls from senior leaders wanting to know how to light a fire under their staff. A study done in Canada between 1984 and 1992 found that the percentage of young people who indicated the importance of hard work dropped from 69 percent to 49 percent.[76]

There are many reasons leaders take a "drifting" approach. Perhaps the mission isn't as compelling, or maybe professionalization has changed the game. Certainly we have been given license to underachieve. Many followers only expect good maintenance, not leadership.

Lack of ambition usually has a "good" excuse. *"The sluggard says, 'There is a lion outside!' or, 'I will be murdered in the streets!'"* (Proverbs 22:13). If the endeavour is bold, they say it is too irresponsible. If it doesn't come easy or requires work, then it is not God's will. They play the "I'm not going to burn myself out" card or proclaim, "I don't want my family to suffer." The truth is, it is good to be tired once and a while.

There are no lazy leaders, just unmotivated and passionless ones. We are never lazy when it comes to the things we want to do. It is not because of a lack of energy, but a lack of motivation. To overcome laziness, we need to find our motivation. If our reason to act is great enough, we will have the will to act.

The Problem of Wrong Ambition

Here are a few verses to consider:

Do nothing out of selfish ambition or vain conceit, but in humility consider others better than yourselves. (Philippians 2:3)

For where you have envy and selfish ambition, there you find disorder and every evil practice. (James 3:16)

The former preach Christ out of selfish ambition, not sincerely, supposing that they can stir up trouble for me while I am in chains. (Philippians 1:17)

Whatever you do, work at it with all your heart, as working for the Lord, not for men, since you know that you will receive an inheritance from the Lord as a reward. It is the Lord Christ you are serving. (Colossians 3:23–24)

Creating Healthy Ambition

1 Thessalonians 4:11 says, *"Make it your ambition to lead a quiet life, to mind your own business and to work with your hands, just as we told you."* I do not mean to be trite or too much a reductionist, but lack of ambition is not a passion problem; it is a spiritual problem.

Major General John H. Stanford survived several tours in Vietnam. He was highly decorated and known for the loyalty he earned from his troops. Stanford then became military traffic management command for the United States Army during the Persian Gulf War. Upon retirement, he took on several noble ventures, with much success. When someone asked him his secret, he responded:

> When anyone asks me that question, I tell them I have the secret to success in life. The secret to success is to stay in love. Staying in love gives you the fire to ignite other people, to see inside other people, to have a greater desire to get things done than other people. A person who is not in love doesn't really feel the kind of excitement that helps them to get ahead and to lead others and to achieve. I don't know any other fire, any other thing that is more exhilarating and is more positive a feeling than love is.[77]

Stay in love with leading! Ambition is an affair not of the head, but of the heart. Keep the fire burning in your belly. Do not become weary in doing well! Love your call to leadership!

26

END

P amela, my sister and personal hero, says on her Facebook page, "Every day is another chance to change your life." However not everyone is going to be thrilled about your new resolve to be secure. In the eyes of the other captives, there is no greater betrayal than for a prisoner to make a run for the wall while others gaze from their cells. Misery loves company, they say. Insecurity is the same. Yet the challenge is to run hard. Run hard anyway. Run alone if you have to. Marathons start and end where the crowds are, but most of a race is run alone. Plenty of great leaders, biblical and otherwise, knew what being alone felt like. Don't worry. It's not a sign of rejection.

Familiarity can be an enemy to a leader's soul. According to an old Japanese proverb, "Even monkeys fall from trees." The jungle, for which they were made, is the same place that can bring injury. The environment to which they are accustomed becomes their foe. We, too, can get used to our habitat and the ease in which we move within it. We coast. Our guard drops. We lean on our competence and success. We've got the jungle well-manicured. Everything runs well, even though we cannot recall what the machine actually does. We are in control, though. We are not moving forward, but at least things are going smoothly. But who wants a life that's always smooth? Those who don't dare to fail greatly never achieve anything great.

Make no mistake. Transformation toward security is not easy, and no one ever reaches security perfection. This is the temptation is to avoid dealing with it. Remember, the journey from insecurity is complex. There isn't a solution that is simple or neat, and the journey to security is never easy. Dr. Chris Thurman wrote:

> Positive results are never easy, no matter how things may appear to be on the surface. If we want anything to be easy, we have to work hard. If we want a quiz to be easy, we have to study hard. If we want a couple of hours on the tennis court to be easy, we have to train hard. If we want our marriages to be easy, we have to work diligently on them. If we want life to be easy, we have to put our all into it, painfully so.[78]

There is no easy pathway to leadership. It is hard work. For some it is harder than others.

I never aspired to be a public communicator, leader, pastor, or visionary, but looking back there was never a moment when I didn't know, deep down, that my future would be in leadership. I was afraid that my skills inventory never matched leadership's demand. I was too scared. But if you are not scared, you are not growing. In a strange way, that fear helped.

I was sitting in my parent's blue 1988 Ford Grand Marquis, waiting in a friend's driveway, when I felt God telling me that ministry was where I needed to be. I had already been accepted to universities for other programs, but there was little doubt in my mind about what my next steps should be.

My first public speaking event was a Sunday evening service at our local church. It was awful. I had fourteen pages of written notes, in red ink, single-spaced. I think the pastor saw the size of my notes and shortened the service to accommodate. Ten minutes after the service started, I was on. Before I could even say a word, my mouth went dry. The piano player handed me a mint and an usher brought me water. I was so embarrassed at the commotion. I read some scripture and set in to my notes. I preached the entire fourteen pages in under eight minutes! Twenty minutes into the service and we were done! Forget about any response time—it was over. The pastor whipped up another message on the spot and preached it just so that the congregants felt like they got a real message.

I walked off the platform humiliated and miserable. I knew as I walked down the center aisle of the church that some crusty old saint would stand up and make me promise to never put people through that again. Sure enough, when I reached the second row, up he stood. But he never rebuked me. He said kind words. And one by one in that small church people gave me compliments. Row by row, the saints of God told lie after lie about what the message meant for them. But herein lies the point. If one person—just one person—had said something discouraging, I would have walked away from it all. Patience and encouragement should be dispensed to everyone freely. It might change their world. It might change the world. Don't let insecurity stop you.

I hope reading these pages has been helpful to you as much as writing them has been helpful to me. Throughout this book, I felt like saying to you, my reader, the words of the Apostle Paul:

> Not that I have already obtained all this, or have already been made perfect, but I press on to take hold of that for which Christ Jesus took hold of me. Brothers, I do not consider myself yet to have taken hold of it. But one thing I do: Forgetting what is behind and straining toward what is ahead, I press on toward the goal to win the prize for which God has called me heavenward in Christ Jesus. (Philippians 3:12–14)

I can only pray now that you and I will increase in our level of security, and consequently our impact for the Kingdom, because of this time together.

You have read this book, and hopefully thought much about yourself and others. You may feel discouraged, but don't turn those feelings into facts. You might have a little homework to do now. As you see some change points in your life do not worry. God always works in you before He works through you. God has the final word. What you think about yourself doesn't matter as much as you think. Do not be dejected by what others may think of you. Os Guinness wrote,

> You may be depressed by the pages of your life that are blotched with compromises, failures, trials, and sin. You have had your say. Others may have had their say. But make no judgments and draw no conclusions until the scaffolding of history is stripped away and you see what it means for God to have had his say—and made you what you are called to be.[79]

I hope you have heard what God thinks of you through our time meandering together through this book's chapters.

Remember, identifying your issues is not the same as changing your issues. Keep at it. If you experience failures and defeats, be assured that you are probably running about average with the rest of us! In fact, you are likely ahead! You may have had some terrible experiences in life, but here you are, reading this book. You're still breathing. You are still sorting out what to do next. Be proud of yourself. You haven't quit. Now your story will have the power to inspire others.

I once had an awkward moment at a church outreach. I pastored in a church that truly wanted to serve and engage its community. Among many other efforts, we would host outreach events in parking lots. There would be free car washes, barbequed food, and activities for kids. On one occasion, the main feature was a local black gospel choir. They were really good. They were a traffic stopper!

In the middle of the choir's set, a mentally disabled young lady moved into the large open area in front of the choir. She began to dance. It was an awkward dance with flamboyant moves that required a lot of space.

Leaders, including me, weren't sure how to respond. We weren't sure how intense this lone dance was going to become. We didn't want our guest choir to feel awkward. We didn't want our community guests to feel embarrassed or sheepish. Should we pull her back? Should we wait it out?

Before we knew what was happening, a distinguished doctor from our assembly walked out of the crowd and tugged at her arm. Surely he was going to politely talk her out of the spotlight. But instead, he started to dance. Hand in hand, they grooved. They danced together in an open parking lot, on a main city street, without a care. While the rest of us were wondering how to control the situation, this man stepped out and danced.

That's a person I want to imitate. I want to be secure like that. I want that freedom from what people think. I covet the ability to be able to step out from the crowd into the wide open space and follow my heart. Maybe if I can do that, others will shed insecurity, too, and join my awkward dance.

But blessed is the man who trusts in the Lord,
whose confidence is in him.
He will be like a tree planted by the water
that sends out its roots by the stream.
It does not fear when heat comes;
its leaves are always green.
It has no worries in a year of drought,
and never fails to bear fruit.
(Jeremiah 17:7–8)

ENDNOTES

1 McGee, Robert S. *The Search for Significance: Seeing Your True Worth Through God's Eyes* (Nashville, TN: Thomas Nelson, 2003), p. 3.

2 Crabb, Jr., Lawrence J. *Basic Principles of Biblical Counseling* (Grand Rapids, MI: Zondervan, 1977), p. 53.

3 Nowinski, Joseph. *Conquering Your Insecurity* (New York, NY: Fireside, 2001) p. 23.

4 Ibid., p. 24.

5 Ogilvie, Lloyd J. *The Bush Is Still Burning* (Nashville, TN: Thomas Nelson, 1985), p. 152.

6 Thurman, Chris. *The Lies We Believe* (Nashville, TN: Thomas Nelson, 2003), p. vii.

7 Kraft, David. *Leaders Who Last* (Wheaton, IL: Good News Publishers, 2010), p. 96.

8 Guinness, Os. *The Call: Finding and Fulfilling the Central Purpose of Your Life* (Nashville, TN: W Publishing, 2008), p. 29.

9   Lawrence, James. *Growing Leaders: Cultivating Discipleship for Yourself and Others* (Peabody, MA: Hendrickson, 2004), p. xvii.

10   Ibid., p. 43.

11   Barna, George, *Revolution* (Carol Stream, IL: Tyndale House, 2005), p. 13.

12   Chambers, Oswald. *My Utmost for His Highest* (Grand Rapids, MI: Discovery House, 1998), p. 42.

13   Kolodiejchuk, Brian. *Mother Teresa: Come Be My Light* (Toronto, ON: Random House, 2007), p. 201.

14   Gallo, Carmine. "Persuading Others to Share Your Vision," *Bloomberg Businessweek Online.* Accessed: September 21, 2007), (http://www.businessweek.com/smallbiz/content/sep2007/sb20070921_254182.htm).

15   Nouwen, Henri J. M. *The Wounded Healer* (Toronto, ON: Random House, 1979), p. 83.

16   Wilder, Thornton. *The Angel That Troubled the Waters, The Collected Short Plays of Thornton Wilder* (New York, NY: Theatre Communciations Group, 1998), p. 74.

17   Kendall, R.T. *God Meant It for Good* (Shippensburg, PA: Destiny Image, 2003), p. 53.

18   This quotation is most often attributed to Charles C. West.

19   Guinness, p.115.

20   Barlow Girl. "I Believe in Love." *How Can We Be Silent?* (Fervent/Spirit-Led, 2007).

21   Twitter. "Rick Warren." Accessed: December 22, 2010 (www.twitter.com/rickwarren).

22 Winter, Richard. *Perfecting Ourselves to Death* (Downers Grove, IL: Inter-Varsity, 2005), p. 126.

23 Burns, Dr. David. "The Perfectionist's Script for Self-Defeat," *Psychology Today* (November 1980), p. 70.

24 McGee, p. ix.

25 Moore, Beth. *So Long, Insecurity: You've Been a Bad Friend to Us* (Carol Stream, IL: Tyndale House, 2010), p. 54.

26 Ibid., p. 279.

27 Cooper, Terry. *Sin, Pride and Self-Acceptance* (Downers Grove, IL: Inter-Varsity, 2003), p. 166.

28 HeinleinRobert A.,*Time Enough for Love (New York, NY: Putnam, 1973), p. 269.*

29 DePree, Max. *Leadership Is an Art* (New York, NY: Doubleday, 1989), p. 92.

30 Creech, Robert, et.al. *The Leader's Journey: Accepting the Call to Personal and Congregational Transformation* (Hoboken, NJ: Jossey-Bass, 2003), p. 18.

31 Maxwell, John. *The Power of Leadership* (Colorado Springs, CO: Honor Books, 2001), p. 92.

32 Moore, p. 19.

33 Statistics Canada (1993). Accessed: August 19, 2010 (www.statcan.gc.ca).

34 McIntosh, Gary L., and Samuel D. Rima. *Overcoming the Dark Side of Leadership* (Grand Rapids, MI: Baker Books, 2007), p. 30.

35 Boyd, Gregory A. *Repenting of Religion* (Grand Rapids, MI: Baker Books, 2004), p. 30.

36 Swindoll, Charles. *Grace Awakening* (Dallas, TX: Word, 1990), p. 129.

37 Perry, Ross. *Thundering Silence* (Belleville, ON: Essence Publishing, 2005), p. 65.

38 The latest estimates from Statistics Canada in 2008 suggest that 38 percent of married couples in Canada will divorce by their thirtieth wedding anniversary (divorce beyond that point is rare). The percentages range from 22 percent in Newfoundland and Labrador to 48 percent in Quebec. In the United States, the figure is 44 percent. (www.canada.com/life/divorce+rate+canada+lower+than+previously+thought/2245611/story.html).

39 I recommend Kevin Leman's book, *The Birth Order Book: Why You Are the Way You Are* (Revell Revised Edition, 2009).

40 Creech, et. al, p. 93.

41 Wikipedia. "Napolean Complex." Accessed: December 19, 2010 (http://en.wikipedia.org/wiki/Napoleon_complex).

42 Nowinski, p. 18.

43 Ibid., p. 19.

44 123Help.Me. "The Negative Effects of False Media Images." Accessed: February 19, 2010 (www.123helpme.com/assets/6396.html).

45 Cursor. "Television and Violence The Scale of the Problem and Where to Go From Here." Accessed: February 19, 2011. (http://cursor.org/stories/television_and_violence.htm).

46 eNotAlone. "Serotonin: From Bliss to Despair." Accessed: August 20, 2010 (www.enotalone.com/article/4116.html).

47 Bennis, Warren. *On Becoming a Leader* (Reading, MA: Addison-Wesley, 1989), p. 67.

48 Lutzer, Erwin W. *After You've Blown It: Reconnecting with God and Others* (Colorado Springs, CO: Multnomah, 2004), p. 5.

49 Thurman, Chris. *The Lies We Believe* (Nashville, TN: Thomas Nelson, 1999), p. 261.

50 Shuddup. "You Spend Your Whole Life Trying to Live Up To What Your Parents Expect to Be." Accessed: September 22, 2010 (www.shuddup.com/people-pages/secret-life/you-spend-your-whole-life%E2%80%A6trying-to-live-up-to-what-your-parents-expect-you-to-be.html).

51 Wikipedia. "Augustine of Hippo." Accessed: September 10, 2010 (http://en.wikiquote.org/wiki/Augustine_of_Hippo).

52 Brown, Steve, *No More Mr. Nice Guy* (Nashville, TN: Thomas Nelson, 1986), p. 47.

53 Kraft, p. 69.

54 Kraft, p.68.

55 This quotation is most often attributed to Dr. Seuss.

56 Guinness, p. 70.

57 Kraft, p. 36.

58 Glasser,William. *Reality Therapy* (Grand Rapids, Michigan: Harper & Row, 1965), p. 10.

59 Farber, Steve. *The Radical Edge* (New York, NY: Kaplan Publishing, 2009), p. iv.

60 Carroll, Lewis. *Alice's Adventures in Wonderland* (Heritage Press, 1941), p. 85.

61   Wikipedia. "The Hedgehog and the Fox." Accessed: January 15, 2011 (http://en.wikipedia.org/wiki/The_Hedgehog_and_the_Fox).

62   Creech, et.al., p. 134.

63   Watterson, Bill. *Calvin and Hobbes* (Kansas City, Missouri: Universal Press Syndicate, 1993).

64   Kolodiejchuk, p. 34.

65   Ibid., p. 196

66   Ibid., p. 324.

67   Blackaby, Henry T., and Richard Blackaby. *Spiritual Leadership: Moving People on to God's Agenda* (Nashville, TN: B&H Publishing Group, 2001), pp. 42–43.

68   Kipling, Rudyard. *The Jungle Books*. p. 96.

69   1 Corinthians 9:19 and Romans 12:10

70   Shaw, George Bernard. *Man and Superman* (Rockville, MD: Wildside Press, 2008), p. 27.

71   This is last stanza of Rudyard Kipling's poem, *L'Envoi*.

72   Roberts, Richard Owen. *Repentance: The First Word of the Gospel* (Wheaton, IL: Crossway Books, 2002), pp. 54, 68, 70.

73   Cordeiro, Wayne. *Leading On Empty* (Ada, MI: Bethany House, 2006), p. 27.

74   Loehr, Jim, and Tony Schwartz. "The Making of a Corporate Athlete," *Harvard Business Review* (January 2001), p. 1.

75 Ford, Leighton. *Transforming Leadership* (Downer's Grove, IL: Intervarsity Press, 1991), p. 193.

76 Statistics Canada (1993). Accessed: February 15, 2011 (www.statcan.gc.ca).

77 Maxwell, John C. *Put Your Dream to the Test: 10 Questions That Will Help You See It and Seize It* (Nashville, TN: Thomas Nelson, 2009), p. 87.

78 Thurman, p. 138.

79 Guinness, p. 232.

8967385R0

Made in the USA
Charleston, SC
30 July 2011